SPARE PARTS FOR PEOPLE

by Margery and Howard Facklam

FROM CELL TO CLONE: The Story of Genetic Engineering
THE BRAIN: Magnificent Mind Machine
CHANGES IN THE WIND: Earth's Shifting Climate

by Margery Facklam

FROZEN SNAKES AND DINOSAUR BONES: Exploring a
  Natural History Museum
WILD ANIMALS, GENTLE WOMEN

Illustrated with photographs and with diagrams by Paul Facklam

SPARE

PARTS

FOR

PEOPLE

Margery and
Howard Facklam

HARCOURT BRACE JOVANOVICH, PUBLISHERS
San Diego   New York   London

Library of Congress Cataloging-in-Publication Data

Facklam, Margery.
   Spare parts for people.

   Bibliography: p.
   Includes index.
   Summary: Discusses current accomplishments in the field of
replacing parts in the human body, including organ transplants, artificial
organs and implants, and artificial joints and limbs.
   1. Artificial organs—Juvenile literature.
   2. Implants, Artificial—Juvenile literature.
   3. Transplantation of organs, tissues, etc.—Juvenile literature.
   [1. Artificial organs. 2. Implants, Artificial.
   3. Transplantation of organs, tissues, etc. 4. Prosthesis]
   I. Facklam, Howard. II. Facklam, Paul, ill.
   III. Title.
   RD130.F33   1987   617'.95   87-8347
   ISBN 0-15-277410-6

Printed in the United States of America
Designed by Michael Farmer
First edition
A B C D E

For Michael Edward Facklam

Contents

Contents

Acknowledgments

Where do you begin when you want to find out what's happening in the complex field of bioengineering? We were lucky to find experts so excited about their work that they opened one door after another for us. We are grateful to each person who took the time to talk with us or write to us about their specialty or experience: Dr. Robert E. Baier, Director of Healthcare Instruments and Devices Institute, SUNY Buffalo; Anne E. Meyer, Surface Science Group, Arvin/Calspan Corporation; Wilson Greatbatch, Clarence, New York; Dr. Irwin A. Ginsburg, Buffalo, New York; Laureen Dunn, Director, Organ Procurement Agency of Western New York; Dr. Don Marshall Gash, Department of Anatomy, University of Rochester Medical School; Dr. Anthony L. Mescher, Department of Anatomy, University of Indiana Medical School; Dr. Louis Cloutier, Burn Treatment Center of Western New York; Dr. William W. Tomford, Massachusetts General Hospital, Department of Orthopaedic Surgery and Rehabilitation Medicine; David Hortman, Buffalo Eye Bank; Dr. Harry E. Flynn, University of Buffalo Dental School; Carol Siyahi, University Communications, Wright State University, Dayton, Ohio, and the late Dr. Ralph Stacy, who was so generous with his time explaining how the rehabilitation program works at Wright State; University of Utah Medical Center; American Council on Transplantation; National Kidney Foundation; National Spinal Cord Injury Association; National Head Injury Foundation; National Research and Resource Facility for Submicron Structures, Cornell University; Sandoz Corporation for information on cyclosporine; 3M for information on the implantable electronic ear; Dr. David K. Halley (F.A.C.S.), Riverside Methodist Hospital, Columbus, Ohio; Edward Hannah, Sr., Columbus, Ohio, recipient of an artificial knee; Sister Mary Yvonne Moran, Louisville, Kentucky, corneal transplant recipient; Patricia DeFries, Derby, New York, heart transplant recipient.

We are especially grateful to Dr. Carmen Privitera, professor of biological sciences at SUNY Buffalo, for his careful review of the manuscript and his thoughtful suggestions.

We appreciate the willingness of these people and the organizations they represent to help us present an honest picture of "spare parts" medicine as it has developed through 1986. Breakthroughs in biologic research and technology will cause dramatic changes in cures and treatments that can make a standard therapy or technique obsolete faster than a book can be written. The challenges are there. We hope that some of the young people reading this book will be challenged to find careers in the exciting fields of biomedical research and development.

No book is produced by writers alone. We are indebted to Anna Bier for her meticulous editing, Paul Facklam for his superb illustrations, and to all the others who took this book from typed pages to the readers' hands.

Margery and Howard Facklam
Clarence Center, N.Y.
1987

SPARE
PARTS
FOR
PEOPLE

1

Mechanical Makeovers

The idea of spare parts for people is not new. Fiction's first bionic men were characters like Captain Hook with his deadly iron claw and Captain Ahab with his whalebone leg. In spite of early attempts to patch broken bodies, glass eyes couldn't see, false teeth didn't fit, and hooks in place of hands probably got in the way as much as they helped.

Even now, with medical technology that seems more like science fiction than fact, there is nothing in reality quite as spectacular as television's Bionic Man or Woman. These fictional characters were miraculous mechanical makeovers who could see through walls with x-ray eyes, lift a truck with an electronic arm, or leap over walls on electronically activated superlegs. No one has found a way to make a real human body better than new. Not yet anyway.

But today's artificial legs don't clomp, and if a hook is used instead of a hand, its electronic controls are so sensitive that it can probably pick up a needle in a haystack. Factories turn out plastic toes, fingers, blood vessels, elbows, knees, hips, and hearts. Surgeons have new tools. Intricate operations are performed with the help of microscopes. Previously hidden parts of the body come to light with bendable fiber optics and miniature TV cameras threaded into the body, and the "bloodless" blades of lasers cut precisely into the target tissue. Doctors can rebuild and reshape bones, skin, and muscle. They can transplant kidneys, livers, lungs, hearts, bones, and teeth. They can restore sight to the blind, sound to the deaf, and movement to the paralyzed. Almost every part of the human body can be reconstructed, repaired, or renovated to some extent.

Replacement parts are both mechanical and organic. An implant is usually a mechanical device like a metal hip, a plastic valve, or an electronic pacemaker. A transplant is a living organ replacing a dying organ—an eye for an eye, a heart for a heart. With the perfected techniques of microsurgery and all its supporting technology, most implants and transplants are successful, for a while at least. The problems tend to arise after surgery when the complications of rejection set in.

The human body doesn't take kindly to invaders. It is a closed territory made up of sixty thousand billion exquisitely designed chemical factories called cells. They work together smoothly until the body is invaded by an alien, which could be a splinter, a virus, or a new heart.

In designing new parts for old bodies, the challenge lies in creating materials that duplicate the natural ones. Very few of the man-made products survive the inner environment of the human body as long or as well as the originals. There is a continual search for materials that won't disintegrate or corrode in the body fluids or cause infection or blood clots. One bioengineer says it's a matter of trying to fool the body into thinking the piece of metal or plastic was there all along. Aluminum, for example, is a sturdy, light-

2

weight metal that might seem perfect for an artificial hip, but it deteriorates and corrodes quickly inside the body.

The whole field of bioengineering exploded when exotic new materials were developed for military uses during World War II and then for the space program that took off during the 1960s and '70s. Some of the metals, ceramics, and plastics that had been created for rockets, space suits, communication systems, or weapons were found to have the qualities needed for use in the human body.

Titanium, for example, is used to build submarines and missiles because it is light but extremely strong. An artificial hip joint must be lightweight, and it certainly has to be strong because even as simple a thing as climbing a flight of stairs presses on the hip joint with a force seven times the body's weight. Since titanium proved to be more biocompatible than aluminum, it has been used as one of the parts of the artificial hip joint.

The clear, strong acrylics such as Plexiglas and Lucite that were developed during World War II proved their worth in the canopies of fighter planes like the British Spitfires. These same plastics are used now to make clear, strong replacement lenses for the human eye. Hundreds of other plastics are used in the spare parts business. Silicones, which survive well and cause no harm in the body, range from water-thin liquids to gels, rubber, and solid resins. They can be molded into shapes for reconstructing a face or replacing a finger. Polyester is made into fibers that can be woven into mesh to support the growth of new tissue or knit into a tube to shore up a vein.

Some repair work merely replaces a part, like a new valve for a damaged heart. Other repairs require miniaturized electronic circuits, like those in artificial limbs, to take over the body's own electrical signals.

One of the most biocompatible substances known is pure carbon, but most available forms of carbon were not strong enough for body parts until the space program developed a carbon that fit the bill. One of its main uses is as an electrical conductor through the skin to stimulate nerve endings that make muscles move. Carbon fibers are made into ribbons that can be woven into the damaged tissue around bones or ligaments. As the carbon fibers form strong bonds with other body chemicals, new tissue grows into the scaffolding of the implanted fibers.

Bioengineers use Velcro patches, silicone valves, acrylic cement, stainless steel rods, and dozens of other materials to build implants. They feed information into computers to design the perfect knee for a football player, or program and pace the movement in the paralyzed muscles of a wheelchair-bound girl.

Although there are heroes and headliners in the spare parts business, it is basically a team event. The highly skilled surgeons who perform the difficult and dramatic surgery make news, but without the inventive biologists, chemists, and physicists who carry out the research and the bioengineers who create and test the devices, we might still be using metal hooks and wooden legs. A doctor often sees the need or has an idea for a device, but it's the bioengineers who do the tinkering.

While surgeons perfect their methods of hooking up a new kidney or lung, biochemists search for more effective drugs that will fool the body's immune system into thinking the new organ is not foreign. Not many years ago it was possible to transplant an organ only from one identical twin to another. Now organ procurement specialists monitor their computers around the clock in a nationwide network that allows them to find a match for most donor organs.

Although the spare parts business is a high-tech industry, it is also an art and a science based on the intricate workings of the human systems. The biggest hurdle lies in beating one of those systems.

2

Beating the System

In almost every old movie there is a scene in which the kindly old family doctor has been keeping watch at the boy's bedside all night. As dawn breaks, the child stirs, opens his eyes, and whispers, "Mommy, I'm hungry."

The doctor says, "The crisis has passed. He's going to be all right."

It may seem corny now, but a scene like this wasn't just some filmmaker's cliché, like the cowboy riding off into the sunset. Before antibiotics, "passing the crisis" was a fact of life. There was little a doctor could do but stand by and wait. The only interchangeable roles were the victim and the disease. The real drama was the battle going on inside the patient. In those days you either got well or you died from diphtheria, smallpox, or one of a dozen other diseases and infections. The outcome depended upon the ability of your immune system to fight the invading germs.

Hundreds of thousands of viruses and bacteria swarm around us constantly, and at any one time the human body harbors some organisms of destruction. Without the immune system, human beings wouldn't last more than a few days. Now and again a child is born without this protective barrier, and the only way he or she can survive is inside a sterile environment. One such "bubble boy" lived for twelve years in a room enclosed in plastic, able to leave it only if he wore a space suit and helmet with its own filtered air supply.

On the surface of each one of the sixty thousand billion cells that make up the human body are molecules that recognize anything foreign, anything not "self." These molecules are called antigens. Destructive bacteria entering the body are immediately recognized as foreign because they have different antigens. Each person has a group of antigens unlike any other. Scientists call them the major histocompatibility complex, which is shortened to MHC. Our MHC is as unique as our fingerprints.

The war between the immune system and the invaders is continual and unending. When the defender wins, the invaders are killed. When the invaders win, the person dies. With a double line of defense and a series of outposts so complex it is far beyond anything that might have been designed by the Pentagon, the immune system works through the bloodstream and its shadow, the lymph system.

When the doctor takes a blood sample and tells you that your white count is high, you know you have an infection of some kind. Your first line of defense, the white blood cells, has gone to work. There are two kinds of white blood cells. The phagocytes are the foot soldiers who meet the enemy head-on. The word phagocyte means "cell-eater," and that's what the white cell does. It fights infection by engulfing the bacteria. When the invaders multiply faster than the phagocytes can eat them, the second kind of white cell, called the lymphocyte, is called into action. Like an elite,

6

highly trained special platoon, lymphocytes patrol the blood and the lymph. Lymph is a colorless fluid that circulates in its own vessels that follow the pattern of the bloodstream. At junctions in the upper chest, the lymph empties into the flow of blood. Like outposts where these moving troops can pick up and send messages, lymph nodes are stationed in the armpits to guard the arms, in the groin to take care of the legs, around the heart, in the throat, and at other strategic spots. Inside about twenty-five feet of the intestinal tract, little clumps of lymph cells called Peyer's patches wage constant battle against the disease-causing bacteria in food that is literally rotting as it is digested.

On these patrols, the lymphocytes not only recognize and destroy the antigens, but they also remember them for the next encounter. Some lymphocytes are made in the bone marrow, so they are called B-cells. B-cells float around until they meet the specific foreign antigen they recognize. That foreign antigen triggers each B-cell to enlarge and divide into a plasma cell and a memory cell. The plasma cells grow, multiply, and produce proteins called antibodies. An antibody is as specific as one key that fits one lock, and it can fight only the antigen that triggered the B-cell into action.

There are a million different kinds of antibodies, and each is "custom-built." It takes four or five days to gear up the body's production line to make enough antibodies to mount a major attack on an invading microorganism. In the fight against some diseases, the patient's fever rages. Finally, when there are enough antibodies to destroy the invaders, the fever breaks, and the crisis has passed. These days there are few long, drawn-out crisis-waiting scenes because an injection of penicillin or one of the other antibiotics comes to the rescue and helps kill off the invading bacteria quickly.

The memory cells produced when the B-cells divided continue to circulate, sometimes providing lifelong immunity against that disease. If you get chicken pox, the antibodies usually last a life-

7

time, and you don't get chicken pox again. Your B lymphocytes remember the chicken pox antigen, and the next time chicken pox organisms attack you, the antibodies kill them before any symptoms of the disease appear. But one cold doesn't make us immune to other colds because cold and flu viruses seem to change and evolve constantly. The antibodies built up during one bout with a cold may not be an exact fit for the antigen of the next strain of cold or flu that comes along.

Most of us were artificially immunized by vaccinations against whooping cough, smallpox, diphtheria, polio, measles, and tetanus when we were very young. Although Edward Jenner is credited with the discovery of vaccination in 1798, he was not the first to try it. In the eleventh century, the Chinese knew that people who survived one attack of smallpox did not usually get the disease again. Throughout China and western Asia there was a kind of primitive way of inoculating people with fluid taken from smallpox patients.

Edward Jenner was not the first person to vaccinate against smallpox, nor did he ever see the microorganism that causes it, but he is credited with the discovery because he published the results of his scientific experiments in 1798. (National Library of Medicine)

Lady Mary Wortley Montagu, who accompanied her husband to Turkey in 1716, was responsible for bringing the idea of inoculations to England. In Constantinople, she had watched a group of old women going from house to house, each carrying nutshells filled with pus taken from people with mild cases of smallpox. These women would scratch a vein in the arm of a "customer," smear some of the infectious fluid on the cut, and then tie the nutshell over the wound. Lady Mary saw these inoculated people fall ill seven or eight days later with mild symptoms of smallpox and then recover in a few days. Not everyone had such a rosy view of the process, however, and other accounts say many people did die, if not directly from the inoculation, probably as the result of an infection from the needle. But Lady Mary was so convinced of the value of the procedure that she inoculated her own three-year-old son. It worked.

When she returned to England and tried to persuade the medical profession to try inoculations, Lady Mary was told it was a "heathen"

Lady Mary Wortley Montagu, who accompanied her husband to Turkey in 1716, watched the crude vaccinations given to children in that country, and she had her own children inoculated by the same method. She returned to England, where she continued to press authorities to inoculate people against smallpox. *(National Library of Medicine)*

procedure. But that didn't stop her. She knew the Prince of Wales, and he made it possible for her to conduct an experiment at Newgate Prison. Six condemned criminals were promised pardons if they would volunteer for inoculation. They did, and all of them survived. Next six orphans were inoculated, and when they recovered from the mild case of smallpox, King George I was so impressed that he ordered the inoculation of his two grandchildren. Although the procedure was never totally safe and no one could predict if a patient would become immune or die, its use spread across Europe and to the young American nation. Many people believed a safer method was necessary, and that's where Edward Jenner came in.

Cowpox in cows is a disease similar to smallpox in people. Farmers knew from experience that anyone who had been infected by cowpox was safe from smallpox. Two cattle breeders, Benjamin Jesty in 1774 and Peter Plett in 1791, were harshly criticized for deliberately infecting their families with cowpox. But during later smallpox epidemics, their families were safe. Neither man, however, got the credit for discovering the vaccination because their results were not published as scientific experiments. Jenner did publish his findings, although he didn't know why the system worked. He had never seen the organism that causes smallpox. We know now that the cowpox antigen is enough like the smallpox antigen to fool the memory cells of the lymphocytes. The cowpox "key" fits the smallpox receptor "lock" on the surface of the cell. Having built antibodies when they were exposed to cowpox, the B-cell lymphocytes are then ready to go into action whenever they meet the similar smallpox antigens.

A second kind of lymphocyte is called the T-cell. It is made in the bone marrow, too, but before it is fully mature, it migrates to a small gland called the thymus, which lies just beneath the breastbone. There the T-cell develops into one of three kinds of "workers," becoming either a "helper," a "killer," or a "suppressor" cell. Each helper lymphocyte is alert to the one specific antigen it was built to recognize as it circulates through the body. Some may go a lifetime without ever encountering their particular foe. But when they do find their matching ragweed pollen or bacteria or transplanted kidney, they begin to reproduce madly at the site of infection. They migrate through the bloodstream to the nearest lymph nodes and the spleen, where they order the killer T-cells to attack.

The killer cells have been off duty, but once on the move they search out the specific antigen receptors on the invading cells. The moment they recognize their antigen, the killer cells bind themselves to the surface of the invader and attack with chemical reactions that break open and kill the foreign cell. The suppressor T-cells are the moderators, keeping both the B-cells and other T-cells from changing or multiplying too much.

In the deadly disease AIDS (Acquired Immune Deficiency Syndrome), these T-cells are overwhelmed, leaving the person with no defense against most infections. It is also the T-cells that go into action against an organ transplant. On the surface of the cells of a transplanted kidney or heart is the MHC signature of the donor. The specific antigens of the donor are the invaders that trigger the T-cells into action against the foreign organ.

The only transplanted organs that are accepted as "self" are those from a recipient's identical twin. Blood, or any tissue or organ from another body, is quickly identified as "not self," and the killer T-cells attack as they would for bacteria or viruses.

We talk about these T-cells sending messages and sending for reinforcements as though they could think. They can't, of course, but on the other hand, neither are they built like little computers or machines. You can't trick a computer. It works on an off-on, yes-no basis. It doesn't yet have a way of evaluating a situation and figuring the best way to handle it. But these lymphocytes do. Not only can they figure out what's happening, but if they are

11

fooled temporarily, they soon change their behavior to attack with a new approach. Lymphocytes seem to learn from experience, and they search for a way around a problem until they find an answer.

In an attempt to get the body to accept someone else's heart or liver or kidney, the doctors try to match as many antigens as possible. Organ matching is based on a scale of A to D. A is a perfect match of at least thirteen different antigens, and D is the poorest match. Because it was so difficult to find healthy donor organs, most early transplants were done with B and C matches, in which only a few of the antigens of the donor matched those of the recipient.

One of the drugs used to try to fool the immune system in the early days of heart transplants was called ALG. During heart surgery on a child, the surgeon would remove a small piece of the thymus gland because a child's thymus is still active. This chunk of tissue was ground up and injected into a horse a little at a time over a period of several days. After six weeks, when the horse's immune system had produced antibodies against this foreign thymus, blood was taken from the horse and refined into a serum the same way serums are produced for inoculations against smallpox and diphtheria. Even with this drug, 85 percent of heart transplant patients died. By the close of 1970, after three years of heart transplants, the American Heart Association reported that of the 166 heart transplants completed around the world, only twenty-three patients had survived.

In that same year, a microbiologist working for a pharmaceutical company in Switzerland went to Norway on vacation. Like many other drug companies, Sandoz Ltd. urges its employees to bring back samples of soil from wherever they go because they are always searching for a new fungus that might work as an antibiotic. (Penicillin came from a fungus in soil, and it caused a major revolution in medicine when Alexander Fleming discovered it in 1928. Bacterial infections caused 25 percent of all deaths until the 1940s, when penicillin finally met standards and went on the market. Now they account for less than 3 percent.)

The dirt from Norway contained a fungus not seen before, and it was called *Trichoderma polysporum*. Tests showed that it produced a protein called cyclosporine, and it was disappointing to find that it had little ability to fight infection. The samples were stuck away on a shelf, out of sight and almost out of mind. But Dr. Jean Borel, chief of immunology at Sandoz, kept going back to study this new protein. In January 1972 he discovered that when cyclosporine was injected into a culture of lymphocytes, it somehow blocked the ability of these immune cells to work, although it didn't kill the lymphocytes. When scientists knew that cyclosporine blocked the T-cell's ability to interfere with communication between the helper and killer cells but did not harm the infection-fighting B-cells, they were sure they had a drug to fight organ rejection.

Before a drug can be sold for general use, it has to be put through a series of tests, first on animals and then on humans. In 1972 cyclosporine was used experimentally in twelve major transplant centers in the United States. Now it is used worldwide as the accepted wonder drug for transplantation. Dr. Norman Shumway, noted heart surgeon at Stanford University, told congressional hearings that he has not had one sign of clinically diagnosable rejection from a heart transplant since he began using cyclosporine in 1980.

That doesn't mean heart transplants work perfectly. There are many other life-threatening problems for the transplant patient, but cyclosporine has become today's "magic bullet," the major breakthrough to a safer way to use nature's own replacement parts. The eventual goal is to create a new generation of drugs that will be able to change the body's response permanently so that the immune system will accept the transplanted organ while it keeps its ability to fight everything else.

Medicine's "magic bullets" have become increasingly more effective since 1910, when the German bacteriologist Paul Ehrlich coined the phrase to describe an arsenic compound he found that killed the deadly syphilis microorganism, and a dye that destroyed the bacteria that caused sleeping sickness. He was also the first to use the word chemotherapy for the practice of using synthetic chemicals to attack specific organisms.

But he probably never imagined a "magic bullet" that would be as versatile or precise or powerful as the newest one, called the monoclonal antibodies. These specially tailored proteins were described by one scientist as comparable to switching from a shotgun to the precision of a rifle bullet. Georges Kohler and Cesar Milstein made the first monoclonal antibodies in their laboratory in Cambridge, England, in 1975.

Although we produce antibodies that specifically match an invading antigen, our immune system sends the whole army of antibodies into action when only one antibody may be needed. Even the serums injected to repel the invading foreign bodies contain a mixed batch of antibodies. Monoclonals are completely different. They are clones, identical descendents of a single cell. They are specific antibodies made to strike a specific target. For the first time, it may be possible to zero in on almost any disorder or to detect almost anything inside the body from a hormone to a poison to a sign of organ rejection. When specially made monoclonal antibodies are mixed with blood from an organ transplant patient, they latch onto the patient's T-cells, which makes the cells easier to count. If there is a sudden increase in T-cells, it may be an early sign of rejection. To counter that rejection, a transplant patient may be given more monoclonals, which will bind with the marauding T-cells, marking them for destruction by the immune system and reversing that episode of rejection.

While some research groups have been developing ways to help the body accept transplants, another team took a giant step toward making a spare part that would not do battle with the immune system. They built an elegantly simple machine called an artificial heart.

3

Heart beyond Repair

Barney Clark was a pioneer and a hero. As surely as any astronaut, this retired dentist set forth into unknown territory when he allowed surgeons to remove his diseased heart and replace it with one made of plastic and metal.

On December 2, 1982, at the University of Utah Medical Center in Salt Lake City, a team of doctors headed by Dr. William C. DeVries placed a "Jarvik-7R" heart in the sixty-one-year-old patient, who would have been dead within the hour without it. It was one day before the fifteenth anniversary of the first human heart transplant. Since then the artificial heart has become more refined and more successful, but on that historic night it was as dramatically daring as the first spaceflight and as long and rigorous in the development.

Almost the biggest hurdle on the way to the successful artificial heart was the idea itself. From the beginning of civilization, the heart has been the symbol of life. Never just a pump, it has worn the label of the brave heart, the loving heart, the broken heart. It took a giant leap over tradition to think of it as merely a pump that could be replaced by a mechanical device.

From the start, researchers knew that an artificial heart must pump at least six quarts of blood per minute, and pump it gently enough to leave blood cells undamaged. It has to fit comfortably in the space left by the removal of the patient's own heart. Made of material that will not promote blood clots or infection, and durable enough to be sterilized, an artificial heart must be absolutely reliable.

A marathon runner or a professional tennis player may have a heart that weighs as much as a pound, but the normal adult heart weighs about eleven ounces. Mostly muscle, it is shaped more like a fist than a valentine.

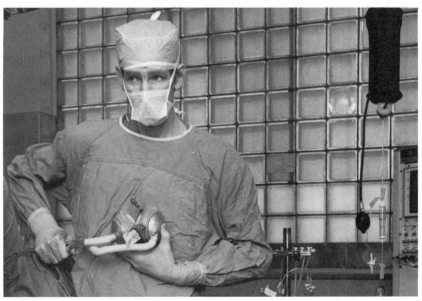

Dr. William C. DeVries holds the Jarvik-7^R heart he implanted in Dr. Barney Clark at the University of Utah Medical Center in 1982. *(University of Utah)*

The human heart has four chambers. The two on top are called atria, and the two that lie below are the ventricles. Valves separate the chambers and regulate the movement of blood from one chamber to another. The atria are mainly reservoirs to collect blood returning to the heart from the veins. The ventricles do the pumping. Most of the work is done by the left ventricle because it is pushing blood into the arteries that feed all the tissues and organs of the body. Less work is done by the right ventricle because it is sending blood under lower pressure to the lungs.

In an average lifetime, the heart beats about three billion times and pumps some fifty million gallons of blood, enough to fill a garden hose stretched around the equator. In 1914, a British physiologist, Ernest Henry Starling, discovered that the body, and not

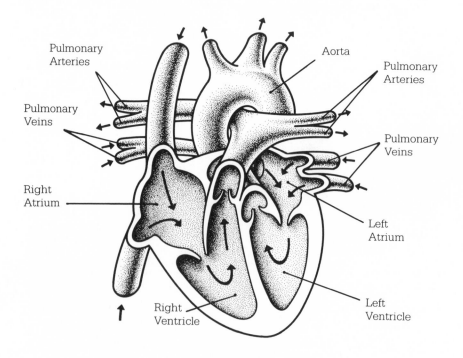

The arrows show the direction of blood flow through the heart.

the heart itself, regulates the work of the heart. When we exercise, we increase the volume and pressure of the blood returning to the heart, which in turn causes the heart to work harder. Known as Starling's Law, this principle means that the amount of blood the heart pumps depends upon the amount of blood the veins return to it. When the body needs more blood, it makes the adjustment by squeezing or expanding the entire network of arteries and veins. The more we exercise, the better this system works. In other words, the heart does the pumping, but the body tells it how much and how fast. This was the basic fact that assured researchers that a mechanical pump could do the work of the natural one.

Dr. Robert Jarvik, who built the artificial heart that bears his name, wrote in *Scientific American:* "When the development of the artificial heart was begun, many people considered the goal unattainable. The natural heart was recognized as a remarkable organ, difficult to duplicate even from the standpoint of durability alone."

But work on it they did. Costing perhaps fifty million dollars and requiring millions of hours of serious scientific time over twenty years, the making of the artificial heart is a story with a cast of characters that includes an inventor/physician who was once turned down for medical school, a young surgeon who practiced sewing plastic hearts into cadavers on his day off, and a calf named Alfred Lord Tennyson.

Heading this cast was Dr. Willem J. Kolff, who had established the first blood bank in Europe and built the first artificial kidney in the Netherlands during the Nazi occupation in World War II. After the war, when he joined the staff of the Cleveland Clinic in Ohio, he turned his considerable talents to work on a heart-lung machine, open-heart surgery, and an artificial heart.

Several early heart designs were powered by electricity. In 1968 the Atomic Energy Commission financed research on a nuclear-powered heart that might operate for up to ten years with no outside support, but it was bulky, expensive, and too complicated. Kolff discussed the problem of a power source for the mechanical heart with some engineers from the National Aeronautics and Space Administration (NASA). They suggested compressed air, which turned out to be simple and practical. Kolff and his associates built a heart made of silicone rubber, driven by compressed air.

In 1967 Kolff moved to the University of Utah as director of its artificial organ program. William DeVries was just finishing his first year of medical school there. After DeVries heard Kolff lecture, he asked him for a job as a research assistant.

"What's your name?" Kolff asked.

"And when I told him," DeVries recalls, "Kolff said, 'That's a good Dutch name. You're hired.' "

When DeVries graduated from medical school, he put in nine years of internship and residency at Duke University before he returned to Utah to start a surgical practice. Still interested in the progress of the artificial heart he had worked on as a research assistant, DeVries worked at least one day a week in Kolff's lab. Before Barney Clark's operation, DeVries had implanted two hundred hearts in calves and sheep, in addition to his practice on human cadavers.

Robert Jarvik is known as a tinkerer and dreamer. By the time he joined Kolff's team at Utah in 1971, he had already patented an automatic suturing device. He got the idea when he watched his physician father in surgery, but he didn't follow his father into medicine after high school. Instead he enrolled in the school of architecture at Syracuse University. When he did decide to try medicine after all, his application wasn't accepted. Like many students in the late sixties, when colleges were crowded, Jarvik applied to and was accepted at a medical school overseas, at the University of Bologna in Italy. Again he dropped out because he found that his real interest was biomechanics. After he graduated from New York University as a bioengineer, he was hired by Dr. Kolff as a

$100-a-week assistant. While he worked on an air-driven artificial heart, Jarvik finished his medical studies at the University of Utah.

One of the problems with the silicone rubber heart was the tendency of the material to cause excessive clotting and uncontrolled bleeding. Jarvik took the problem to specialists in surface energy. Dr. Robert E. Baier and Anne E. Meyer in the surface science section of the Calspan Corporation explain surface energy as the place where "the rubber meets the road, or in the case of

In the surface science laboratory of Calspan Corporation, Anne E. Meyer and Dr. Robert E. Baier look at an artificial heart sac and an artificial hip implant they worked on. *(Calspan Corporation)*

the heart, where the blood meets the plastic." Low surface energy is what makes things not stick to Teflon.

There are times when it's important to have an implant stick. An artificial hip or a tooth must hold fast and not slip. But for an artificial heart, it was essential to find something to make the surface unstickable. Many of the mechanically good materials caused thromboses—blood clots. Someone had the idea that if a fuzzy layer of Dacron fibers could be laid down first, the clots would be encouraged to stick. The idea was if the blood was going to clot, let it. It was hoped that a natural protective layer would form and that the blood would flow smoothly over it. But the clotting continued to build up, clogging the trial hearts.

Dr. Baier says that they had to remember that nature uses "primer coats." A layer of protein sticks to every surface—blood, bone, or any tissue. You can feel this coating on your gums and teeth. The standard response of the body to any foreign tissue is a quick cover of protein. Finally, engineers learned to coat the inside of the artificial heart with an almost miraculously thin skin of a liquid elastic, which is a marriage of silicone rubber and Biomer, a medical grade of the Lycra fabric used to make "living" bras and girdles.

One of Jarvik's Biomer-lined hearts was implanted in a calf named Alfred, Lord Tennyson. The morning after surgery, the calf was on its feet, munching on grain, watched over by the affectionate "calf sitters." His blood pumped normally, and he continued to eat, sleep, and exercise comfortably on a treadmill for 268 days, when his body outgrew the artificial heart. Sheep are often used now to test the plastic pumps because their bodies are closer to human size.

Without research on animals, there would be no progress in medicine. Skilled veterinarians are a vital part of the research team. It was one of the veterinarians at Utah Medical Center, Dr. Donald Olson, who came up with the lifesaving idea of leaving the natural heart's aortic and pulmonary valves in place when an artificial

— Left Heart Sac
— 103 days
— Calf #36, "Clancey II"

A calf named Clancey II lived with this artificial heart for 103 days. After the calf died, surface science engineers studied the heart and found ways to reduce clotting with changes in design and materials. *(Calspan Corporation)*

heart is attached. Survival time improved tremendously because less can go wrong with natural valves than with artificial ones.

Every biomedical device has to go through stages: laboratory development, testing on animals, and then testing on humans, always starting with the high-risk people. "It's a situation born to fail," says Anne Meyer. "We must work with people in a situation of either you give them a heart or they're dead. Worst-case patients first. After you show magic and miracles you're allowed to go to other people."

Heart disease is the leading cause of death in the United States. In spite of information about smoking, high blood pressure, too little exercise, obesity, and stress—information that could cut the death rate by 25 percent—more than a million people are stricken by heart disease each year. There is a battery of drugs that help and dozens of surgical procedures to sew up holes, bypass diseased arteries, repair damaged valves or insert pacemakers, but when all treatments fail, only a new heart will do.

Patients have lived more than ten years with transplanted human hearts, but healthy hearts are not, as one surgeon says, lined up waiting on a store shelf. An artificial heart can buy time for a patient. It can serve as a temporary pump until a matching donor heart is found. For patients like Barney Clark, who was too ill to respond favorably to a transplant, the artificial heart was the only hope.

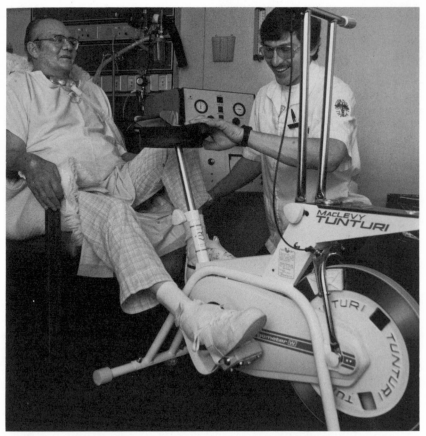

Dr. Barney Clark exercising after his heart implant. *(Brad Nelson, University of Utah)*

At first the University of Utah was authorized by the Food and Drug Administration (FDA) to use the experimental artificial heart for people who would otherwise die on the operating table during heart surgery. Before they had such a patient, Dr. Denton Cooley at the Texas Heart Institute implanted an artificial heart similar to the Jarvik-7^R in a thirty-six-year-old bus driver who could not be revived after bypass surgery. Cooley did not have FDA authorization, but he kept his patient alive until a donor heart was found two days later. Finally, the FDA guidelines were changed to include those with progressive heart failure.

Barney Clark's feeble, quivering heart was badly damaged and failing from a disease called cardiomyopathy, which doctors suspected was caused by a viral infection. Too old to qualify for a human heart transplant and too sick to respond to further drug therapy, Clark opted for the plastic heart. He signed an eleven-page consent form twice, once when he entered the hospital and again the next day to show he had not changed his mind or misunderstood the trial ahead. The form let him know that the ventricles from his own heart would be removed and that a mechanical heart device would be placed in his chest in the space formerly occupied by his own natural heart. It told him that the mechanical device would require his body to be attached by two plastic six-foot-long air tubes to an air-driving system to pump his blood through his mechanical heart and circulate it through his body. Everything was described; nothing was left out except, of course, what could not be known about the rocky recovery days ahead.

Dr. DeVries, who had rehearsed his surgical group until they performed with the precision of a military drill team, cut away the two lower chambers of Clark's heart, the ventricles that pump the blood. He left in place the atria, which act as reservoirs to receive blood from the body and send it to the ventricles at the proper moment. Next he stitched Dacron fittings onto the atria and the two major blood vessels, the aorta and the pulmonary artery to the lungs. Like lids on tight-fitting Tupperware, the Jarvik-7^R ventricles were snapped into place on the Dacron fittings and held together with Velcro patches. With this kind of connection, the ventricles could be changed or repositioned quickly without restitching. The pump was turned on. Puffs of air from the compressor, driven by the 375-pound power unit, pushed against diaphragms in the ventricles and forced blood out into the body.

When the puffs of air stopped, the ventricles refilled with blood. Immediately Clark's blood flow rose from a quart to a normal six

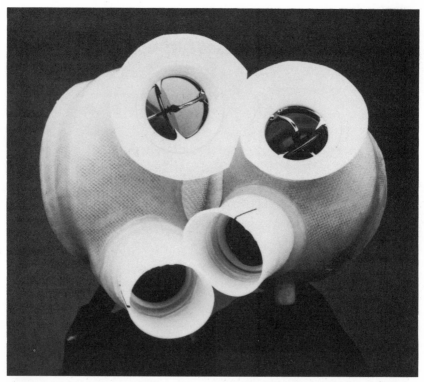

The Jarvik-7^R artificial heart consists of two separate ventricles with air chambers. In order to implant the heart, the ventricles from the natural heart are surgically removed. The remaining atria are sewn to the polyester velour cuffs, which are then snapped onto the artificial heart. Connections to the pulmonary artery and the aorta are also stitched in place, using woven polyester grafts. You can see the titanium and pyrolytic carbon valves that ensure smooth, one-direction blood flow. *(JARVIK-7^R Total Artificial Heart)*

quarts per minute, and his blood pressure was that of an eighteen-year-old. He had become the first person in history to have completely adjustable blood pressure and heart rate.

Eventually, a combination of effects from diabetes and lung disease that had ravaged his body for years killed Barney Clark, but at the end of his courageous 112 days, the Jarvik-7^R heart was still beating.

DeVries's second artificial heart patient, William Schroeder, survived twenty-one months, during which he suffered a series of damaging strokes from blood clots that formed around the heart's valves.

Five artificial hearts have been implanted within three years, and another three have been used temporarily while the patients waited

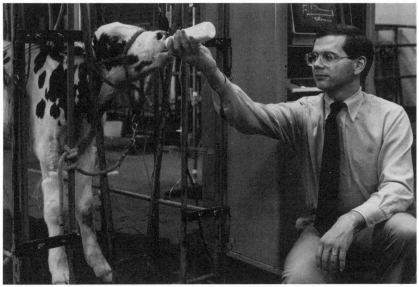

Johnny, a two-month-old bull calf, was the smallest calf ever to receive a total artificial heart designed to fit a small man or woman. The 117-pound Holstein recovered quickly with the new heart, called the Utah 100. It is elliptical—longer, thinner, and narrower than the Jarvik-7^R implanted in Dr. Barney Clark. Kevin Murray, M.D., who is feeding Johnny, says the heart is an excellent fit and is small enough not to interfere with the lungs or large blood vessels. *(Brad Nelson, University of Utah)*

for human transplants. New and improved designs have cut down on the debilitating strokes. One newer model, called the Utah 100, is more elliptical than the Jarvik-7^R and seems to fit better into the chest. A heart built at Pennsylvania State University has two advantages, a seamless lining expected to reduce the risk of blood clots, and the ability to adjust automatically to changes in the user's activities. Barney Clark's heart rate had to be adjusted manually when he sat up or moved around.

The artificial heart will become more efficient, more reliable, less cumbersome, and safer. It won't be long before the patient will wear a lightweight power pack on a belt to drive a small compressor, instead of being attached to one the size of a washing machine. Eventually a totally implantable heart may be built with an internal power source. But most surgeons think the artificial heart's primary use will be as a stopgap, a temporary pump to use until a human donor heart is found, or perhaps until the patient's own heart heals.

The artificial heart is the single most expensive medical procedure, costing more than $250,000. Who will get it? And who will decide? Will it go only to the person who can afford it? Or will it be, like kidney transplants and kidney dialysis, paid for through government funding?

Jarvik says that the artificial heart must be more than a pump. "It must also be more than functional, reliable, and dependable. It must be forgettable."

4

New Hearts for Old

Heart transplants no longer make headlines. They are front-page news only when they involve a first . . . a new technique, the youngest patient, or perhaps the most unlikely combination of donor/recipient, like the California teenage girl who received the heart of her boyfriend who had willed it to her when he had a premonition of his death.

Headlines or not, the transplantation of a heart is a stunning performance. Like the implant of the artificial heart, the first transplant required a level of courage, skill, and determination beyond almost any medical feat.

On December 3, 1967, at the Groote Schuur Hospital in Cape Town, South Africa, Dr. Christiaan Barnard removed the heart from twenty-five-year-old Denise Darvall, who had died in a car crash. Waiting in the adjoining operating room was fifty-three-year-old Louis Washkansky, whose damaged heart was about to quit. Barnard and his team had trained for years for this tense moment when all the circumstances were right for a transplant.

But think back even further and imagine the tension surrounding the operating table when the very first surgeon was daring enough to touch a living, pulsing heart. That was 1891, and the patient was a twenty-two-year-old man who had been stabbed in the chest. The surgeon was H. C. Dalton, a professor of surgery in St. Louis when he stitched up the membrane (pericardium) that covers the heart. Two years later in Chicago, the well-known black surgeon Daniel H. Williams also sewed a stab wound in a twenty-two-year-old man. Both patients survived. But neither of these operations invaded the heart itself, and most surgeons believed it was best not to try.

In 1896, Stephen Paget wrote a book called *The Surgery of the Chest* in which he said, "The surgery of the heart has probably reached the limits set by nature to all surgery; no new method and no new discovery can overcome the natural difficulties that attend a wound of the heart." But that same year, in Frankfurt, Germany, Dr. Ludwig Rehn performed the first successful suture of living human heart muscle, and it marked the beginning of dramatic changes in cardiac surgery. Other cases were reported in Europe soon after, but the first American doctor to stitch the heart muscle was Dr. Luther Hill of Montgomery, Alabama, in 1902. His patient was a thirteen-year-old boy who had been stabbed in the chest five times, and it's hard to imagine a worse time or place for surgery. Lighted by two kerosene lamps, the successful operation took place on a wooden kitchen table in an old shack.

Even though the name of one person goes into the history books as the inventor or discoverer, not one new technique, process, or piece of equipment is born alone. Before any dramatic medical procedure, there are many steps and a long list of people who helped. Wilhelm Roentgen's discovery of x-rays in 1895 greatly improved and simplified the diagnosis of heart disease. Lord Joseph Lister's introduction of aseptic techniques in the 1860s "succeeded in converting hospitals into something more than elaborate pauses on the way to the grave," according to science writer Isaac Asimov.

The compact electrocardiograph machine, commonly used as part of a checkup or in the diagnosis of heart disease, traces the electrical activity of the heart on a graph. The first one was built in the early 1900s, when Dr. Willem Einthoven constructed a working EKG machine that weighed six hundred pounds and took up two rooms. But the three crucial developments that opened the way to successful heart surgery more than almost any others were thoracic anesthesia, blood transfusions and blood banks, and anastomosis, or a way to sew blood vessels together without leaking.

The history of blood transfusions covers centuries of trial and error, beginning in 1615 with the first description of human blood transfused into a man. So much had to be learned—how to keep the blood from clotting, how to recognize the types of blood in order to avoid clumping of the red blood cells, and how to preserve the blood in storage. Over and over, in the stories about the people whose work built step by step toward today's successful methods of blood transfusions and blood banks, there is an underlying sense of courage to try and to learn from the failures.

Stitching together two blood vessels so they don't leak doesn't sound like much of a problem, but the technique has been called one of the great surgical achievements of the early twentieth century. Using fine needles and suture thread, Alexis Carrel in 1902 found a way to sew blood vessels together end to end with as few as three stitches. His technique was a byproduct of his main interest in transplanting organs because he had to have a blood supply in the organ's new location. Although Carrel's careful suturing didn't bring about organ transplants directly, he continued his research by trying to keep organs alive by means of passing blood or some substitute through the organ's own blood vessels. The process is called perfusion, and it's essential in both the artificial kidney and in heart surgery. He kept a chicken heart alive in this way for thirty-four years, which is much longer than a chicken's life span. With the aviator-hero-inventor Charles Lindbergh, Carrel built a germ-proof perfusion pump that became known as an "artificial heart."

Even with all these developments, no one had actually been inside the heart to repair holes and valves. That kind of open-heart surgery had to wait for even further developments. The big breakthrough was the heart-lung machine, which detoured the blood from the patient into a machine that fed it fresh oxygen and returned the blood to the body without going through the heart and lungs. Again, dozens of people and hundreds upon hundreds of experiments played a part in the making of such a machine. One of the famous names in this field is John H. Gibbon, Jr., who began to work on a heart-lung machine in 1934 at Massachusetts General Hospital in Boston. On May 6, 1953, Gibbon operated on an

In 1902 Alexis Carrel developed a technique in which he stitched blood vessels together end to end with as few as three stitches and with no leaks. This practical development made possible the repair and replacement of blood vessels and the transplantation of organs. He was awarded the Nobel Prize in medicine and physiology for this work in 1912. *(National Library of Medicine)*

eighteen-year-old girl with congestive heart failure. It was the first successful open-heart operation with total heart-lung bypass, and it set the stage for heart repairs we now take for granted. It also set the stage for that first heart transplant in South Africa and for the hundreds that have followed.

The first heart transplant patient, Louis Washkansky, lived only twelve days with his new heart because he had been in such poor health before the surgery and because his body rejected the donor heart. But in the next year, 1968, there was a burst of transplant surgery. At Stanford University, Dr. Norman Shumway performed the first such operation in the United States, and since then Stanford has become one of the leading centers for heart transplants, holding the longest survival record of twelve years.

A heart is transplanted as a last resort. By 1985, 635 transplants had been performed in the United States, with a one-year survival rate of 80 percent. It's an accepted fact that the surgical techniques and support systems for heart transplants work. But what of the patient?

When twenty-two-year-old Pat DeFries from Derby, New York, went to the hospital for gall bladder surgery, she did not suspect that she would soon be waiting for a new heart. Although she was aware of a family history of cardiomyopathy, her symptoms were apparently masked by other problems. When her doctor told her she would have to have a transplant, she was stunned.

"It didn't occur to me to say no. I wanted to see my two children grow up. But the waiting is the worst part," Pat said. "First you go through all the red tape while the hospital tries to find the funding to pay for the operation. They have to fill in stacks of forms about the expected success rate in order to get a grant. I was lucky because I'd been in the Army, and the Veterans Administration covered the costs. But the emotional ups and downs are unreal. You find yourself waiting for weekends and holidays because there are more car accidents then. I know it sounds terrible, but all you can think of is that your heart is dying, and someone else has to die for you to live."

Pat waited sixty-eight days. She was first on the computer list, but two older men got hearts before she did because of better tissue matches. She remembers nothing of the surgery itself, of course, and very little immediately afterward because she was on medication. But in a few days she began to feel wonderful, better than she had ever felt before.

Once a month she went in for a biopsy. "That's pretty bad, too," Pat says. A tiny piece of her new heart is snipped off by a tiny blade threaded through a catheter passed from either her groin or her neck by way of a vein. Because she felt so well, she was unprepared for the devastating news that her immune system was rejecting the new heart. "I take cyclosporine every day, and I will every day of my life. I can't even describe the taste. It's oily, but much worse than cod-liver oil, and it coats your teeth." She shudders as she describes it. "The cyclosporine increases blood pressure, so I take medication for that, and several other things as well." When the rejection started, the treatment was agonizing. Added steroids made her joints extremely painful, and her body became bloated.

But that's past, and except for a biopsy once every three months now, her new heart has been beating comfortably for two years. She knows who the donor is because someone sent her a newspaper clipping about a man who died in a crash in Syracuse, New York, that weekend, and the article said his heart had been sent to a woman at the Veterans Administration hospital in Buffalo. Pat is grateful for his gift of life to her, and she thinks of him almost daily, but she doesn't think of her heart as separate from herself. It's hers.

Would she try an artificial heart if it became necessary? Pat says no. "Quality of life is important, and I don't think I'd want to live as Bill Schroeder and the others have. I'd let them use it temporarily if I had to wait for another transplant, maybe."

34

Mary Gohlke, who was the first person to have both heart and lungs transplanted at one time, agreed with Pat. She was grateful for the organ donation, for the great skill of Dr. Shumway at Stanford, and for the awful but wonderful drug, cyclosporine. Not only did Mary have to wait an agonizingly long time for donor organs, but she had a frustrating wait for the FDA to authorize the use of cyclosporine. It had been okayed for use in heart transplants only, but after Mary's personal campaign, it was taken off the experimental list and allowed for all transplant surgery.

A human heart is expensive; it may be rejected; it requires waiting for another person to die; but once in place, it beats like one's own.

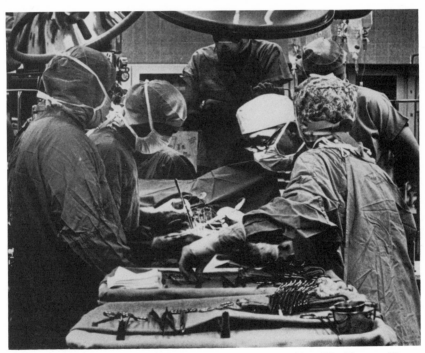

At Stanford University in March 1981, Dr. Bruce Reitz *(left)* and Dr. Norman Shumway performed the first heart-lung transplant. *(Chuck Painter, News Service, Stanford, CA)*

5

Setting the Pace

Fortunately, most heart problems don't require treatment as drastic as the artificial heart or transplants; they can be controlled by exercise, healthy diet, and medication. Others may require a new valve, a replaced artery, or a pacemaker.

Wilson Greatbatch invented the first clinically successful self-powered implantable heart pacemaker in 1960, but he knew in 1951 that he could make one. As one of the thousands of World War II veterans returning to college under the G.I. bill, Greatbatch was a student at Cornell University. He was working as an electronics technician in one of the college labs to support his family when he met two brain surgeons on summer sabbatical who were studying new surgical techniques.

"The surgeons carried their lunches in brown bags, as I did," Greatbatch says, "and noontimes we would sit on the grass in the bright Ithaca sun and talk shop. I learned much practical physiology from them. The subject of heart block came up. When they described it, I knew I could fix it, but not with the vacuum tubes and storage batteries we had then."

He learned that the heart has its own built-in pacemaker. The rhythmic contractions and relaxations of the whole mass of heart muscle are paced by a group of specialized tissue cells that start an electrical impulse that spreads over the heart from one cell to another. If the heart's own pacemaker fails, the beat becomes erratic. Not enough oxygen gets to the body, and the heart muscle tires from the struggle. It's called a heart block.

Even after graduation, when Greatbatch went to work at Cornell Aeronautical Laboratory in Buffalo, New York, he kept the idea of a pacemaker always in mind. He did not know that Dr. Paul Zoll in Boston was building the first of his historic external pacemakers. It's not unusual for several people to be trying to solve the same problem at the same time. The one who is credited with the discovery or invention is the one who gets the patent or publishes the information first.

One day in 1956, when the first really commercial silicon transistors had become available, Greatbatch was building equipment for a doctor who wanted to record fast heart sounds. He reached into his resistor box but misread the colors and picked up a brown-black-green resistor instead of the brown-black-orange one he meant to use.

According to Greatbatch: "The circuit started to 'squeg' with a 1.8 millisecond pulse, followed by a one-second quiescent interval. During the interval, the transistor was cut off and drew practically no current. I stared at the thing in disbelief and then realized that this was exactly what was needed to drive a heart. I built a few more. For the next five years, most of the world's pacemakers were to use [this] oscillator . . . just because I grabbed the wrong resistor."

At first Greatbatch could not interest any doctors in a pacemaker that could be implanted in the patient's chest. Then one day in the spring of 1958, he visited Dr. William C. Chardack, who was chief of surgery at the Veterans Administration hospital in Buffalo, New York. When Greatbatch described his pacemaker, Dr. Chardack walked up and down the lab a couple of times. Then, says Wilson Greatbatch, "He looked at me strangely and said, 'If you can do that, you can save ten thousand lives a year.' Three weeks later we had our first model in a dog."

With $2,000 in cash and enough saved to feed his family for two years, Greatbatch quit his job. "I gave the family money to my wife. I then took the $2,000 and went up into my wood-heated barn workshop. In two years I built fifty pacemakers, forty of which went into animals and ten into patients. We had no grant

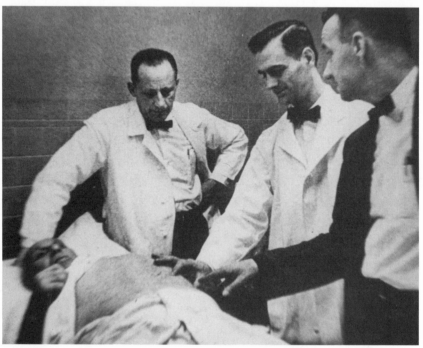

Dr. William C. Chardack, Dr. Andrew Gage, and Wilson Greatbatch called themselves the "bow tie" team in 1960 after they had implanted their first successful pacemaker.

funding and asked for none. The program was successful. We got fifty pacemakers for $2,000. Today, you can't buy one for that."

During 1960, Greatbatch handmade dozens of pacemakers, and Dr. Chardack and his associates implanted ten successfully in patients. Twenty-five years later, one of those patients, still using a pacemaker at the age of eighty, attended a dinner honoring Greatbatch as "Engineer of the Year." At first, it was optimistically estimated that perhaps 10,000 pacemakers might be used in a year. Now more than 300,000 people each year are equipped with implanted pacemakers.

The early pacemakers were large and clumsy compared to the miniaturized versions made now. "We were pretty naive about pacemaker designs," says Greatbatch. "We originally thought that wrapping the module in electric tape would seal it. We soon found that *any* void would fill with fluid, and we began to cast our electronics into a solid epoxy block."

"The warm, moist environment of the human body proved a far more hostile environment than outer space or the bottom of the sea. We had predicted a five-year pacemaker in our first 1959 paper. Even by 1970 we were only getting two years!" Greatbatch wrote.

The pacemaker is implanted just under the skin, usually in the chest just below the collarbone. Although it's not rejected as an organ might be, the pacemaker can corrode and deteriorate in the hostile environment of the human body and cause infection if it isn't made of the proper biocompatible materials and adequately sterilized before use.

More years of work went into finding better materials and designs. Greatbatch joined with Medtronics, a small company then operating from a garage in Minneapolis. Earl Bakken, with the advice of heart surgeon C. Walton Lillehei, had been making external, hand-held pacemakers. From them Greatbatch learned about silicones and medical adhesives.

Even when the pacemakers were sealed in silicone, some of them developed leaks. One step in a rigorous series of tests for the pacemakers, including exposure to heat and cold, was a shock test that Greatbatch worked out at his home before shipping pacemakers on to Minneapolis. "I had two ovens set up in my bedroom," he explains. "My wife did much of the testing. The shock test consisted of striking the transistor while under test with a wooden pencil, while measuring beta (current gain). We found that a metal pencil could wreck the transistor, but a wooden pencil could not. Many mornings I would awake to the cadence of Eleanor tap, tap, tapping the transistors with her calibrated pencil. For some months every transistor that was used worldwide in Medtronic pacemakers got tapped in my bedroom."

Although the components became more reliable, the batteries limited the life of the pacemakers. Nuclear batteries, rechargeable batteries, and biological batteries were tried, but the group finally settled on the lithium battery, which is still used because it is so reliable.

Today's pacemaker works on demand. It "listens" to the heart, and instead of sending signals continually, it kicks in when it senses the need. Newer models are computerized with as many as a hundred thousand transistors on a single chip no larger than a fingernail. They have memories that can store and summarize such things as the patient's name, pacemaker model, date of implant, and even a summary of the number of times the demand function was used in the preceding six months.

Another kind of pacemaker was a spin-off from the space program's miniaturized circuitry. Called the implantable automatic cardioverter-defibrillator, it was designed to correct ventricular fibrillation, a condition in which the heart loses its ability to pump blood, causing death or brain damage in a matter of minutes. This device monitors the heart, and when it senses the onset of this break in rhythm, it delivers a shock to restore the normal beat.

It's a miniaturized version of the defibrillators used by emergency squads.

To expect an engineer to build a valve that will hold up through thirty-five million openings and closings each year and that will be accurate enough to regulate the flow of fluid through some 12,000 miles of arteries, veins, and capillaries is asking for miracles. Not only do our heart valves open and close 100,000 times a day, year in and year out for eighty years or more, but they are self-repairing, up to a point. Deterioration from aging or rheumatic fever or other diseases causes wear and tear on the valves. Sometimes they don't make a tight seal; one will fail to open or close in its proper sequence. Blood with less oxygen gets pumped around in such cases, and the whole body suffers.

The replacement of heart valves is a fairly routine operation now. The first artificial valve was built by an aerospace engineer, M. Lowell Edwards, and a heart surgeon, Dr. Albert Starr, at the University of Oregon Medical School in Portland, and tested by a team at Harvard Medical School in 1960. It was a ball-and-cage gadget that worked much like the ball that seals a snorkel to keep water out when you dive. The Teflon ball moved freely in a cage made of three strands of titanium wire attached to a rim like a hat. The valve was stitched into the heart with Dacron thread.

Like all implanted parts, the valve has gone through many designs and many materials to avoid the clotting that is always the danger. The valves used in the artificial heart are pyrolytic carbon discs that tilt up and down to allow blood to flow from the atrium into the ventricle. As the ventricle fills, the rising blood pushes the disc shut. (See the illustration on page 42.)

In affluent countries where people eat a diet rich in fats, a common heart problem stems from arteries clogged with cholesterol. When the problem gets severe enough, it sometimes can be corrected by cleaning out the artery or putting in a new artery as a detour for the clogged one. This kind of detour, called bypass

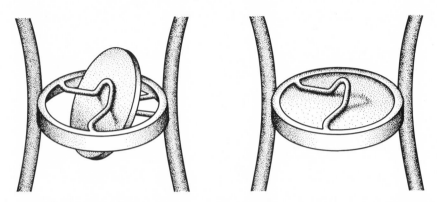

An artificial mitral valve used between the left atrium and the left ventricle consists of a plastic disc between two struts of wire. The valve allows blood to flow from the atrium into the ventricle but closes when the ventricle fills with blood, preventing a backflow of blood into the atrium.

surgery, is so common that it's not unusual to hear people brag, "Oh, I've had a double bypass, or a triple bypass."

The best of all replacements for an artery is, of course, a human artery or vein, and for many years the saphenous vein of the leg was used. But that requires double surgery. The vein must be removed from the leg and replaced in the repair site. The next best and most common replacement blood vessel is a woven or knitted tubing of Dacron, nylon, or Teflon fibers.

The doctors Herbert and Irving Darvik, of Englewood, New Jersey, had been using these fabric arteries for many years, but they were discouraged by the knowledge that when they put in an artificial graft, they were likely to have that patient back in a few years with more clots. Then they began experimenting with a substitute vein that was being thrown into hospital incinerators every day—the human umbilical cord. The Darviks found that it worked perfectly in place of damaged blood vessels. Bioengineer Dr. Robert Baier, who helped the Darviks perfect the umbilical cord graft, says it is as efficient as a garden hose. It's not necessary to match tissue types. It is blood compatible for nine months, and it won't cause clotting. It's straight, tough, and resilient. When it's properly prepared, it can be packed in saline and alcohol and stored on a shelf until needed. After a baby is born in one of the hospitals in the collection area of New Jersey, parts of New York State, and Europe, a nurse rinses the cord, puts it in a Ziploc bag, and throws it in the freezer. The cords are picked up each week and shipped in refrigerated boxes to the New Jersey factory, where each cord is carefully checked for defects.

Although there are three blood vessels in an umbilical cord, only the large vein is used; the two smaller vessels are being tested for replacements where smaller-sized tubes are needed. A rod called a mandril is slipped through the cord to keep it from collapsing while it is cross-linked, which is a process like the tanning of leather, to keep it from deteriorating.

A surgeon can order the cords in varying lengths. Six women, trained at the factory for six months, learned anastomosis, which is the surgeon's term for the precise stitching together of blood vessels. Because rough sutures or stitches can provide a place for a blood clot to form, it is essential that the seams be as smooth as possible.

Blood transfusions are so common that we seldom think of them as organ transplants, but that is, of course, what they are. We so take them for granted that we forget, too, how hard pressed blood banks are to keep adequate supplies on hand, especially rare types such as AB negative. Blood substitutes, such as one called Fluosol, are still in the experimental stage. Fluosol is made from fluoro-carbons, which are chemicals that won't combine with any other chemicals under most circumstances, and they won't be rejected because they are not proteins. This bionic blood can be injected into the bloodstream to carry oxygen until the body can replenish its own supply of red blood cells. It can be used to maintain blood pressure and blood volume temporarily, and it is especially effective as a way of delivering certain kinds of drugs into the body.

What will they think of next?

6

Fixing the Filter
and the Factory

On a morning in October 1985, while twenty-three-year-old Raymond Shriver was having a kidney transplant at Children's Hospital in Buffalo, New York, his twenty-one-year-old sister Doreen was in the adjoining operating room, also receiving a healthy kidney. The news reports that day centered around two facts: the kidneys were from a single donor, and the transplant surgeons were identical twin brothers. Without the unusual cast of characters, these operations probably would have gone unnoticed because kidney transplants have become so common.

Of the 6,968 kidney transplants reported by the American Council on Transplantation in 1984, 96 percent of them worked. Success generally means that the patient lived at least one year after the transplant. Such a high rate of success did not come easily, or without years of research. The first step was finding out how the kidneys work.

All the systems of the body are constantly adjusting in order to stay on an even keel. But it is the bean-shaped, fist-sized pair of kidneys that is responsible for the major job of balancing what comes in with what goes out. The kidneys are forever filtering and fixing to maintain the delicate balance of internal fluids and salts. This balance is called homeostasis. The blood is like a warehouse stocked with red and white cells, antibodies, platelets, hormones, proteins, salts, and nutrients, as well as waste products. And whether we eat five chocolate chip cookies and a slice of pizza or drink only a glass of water, whether the demand for energy is only a low level for watching TV or a great surge for playing a set of tennis, the body's chemistry must stay balanced within a very narrow limit.

The glucose in your blood, for example, is normally about seven parts in 10,000, but if it goes up to twelve and stays there, you are diabetic. If it drops to three, you may die. There is only a trace of calcium in normal blood, one part in 10,000, but a drop to half that amount causes convulsions and death. A radical drop in the level of potassium can cause paralysis; breathing stops and you may die. But if potassium rises, the heart may beat erratically, which can also lead to death.

No matter how many pretzels you eat or how heavily you salt your food, the amount of sodium (salt) in your bloodstream does not change more than 3 percent. The kidneys keep track of all these chemicals. They are programmed to know exactly how much of each should be in the blood, and they regulate the balance by constantly filtering about 500 gallons of blood each day.

The filtration system in a pair of kidneys is made up of two million nephrons, which, laid end to end, would stretch seventy miles. Each nephron is a microscopic filter with a tangled tuft of capillaries called a glomerulus, surrounded by a capsule attached to a long, coiled tubule. From the 500 gallons of blood that pass through the glomeruli, about 50 gallons of liquid called plasma are filtered out. When the plasma goes through the tubules, most of its contents are reabsorbed back into the bloodstream, and what's left over is about a quart of urine. The dirty blood full of waste products goes into the nephrons; clean blood and urine come out.

Kidneys work on the "soup-making" principle. If too many carrots or onions are dumped into a pot of soup, it's easier to filter them all out and put back what you want than to try to scoop out the right amount of each ingredient. It's more efficient for kidneys to filter everything. A filter that would leave in only what's right for the body's chemical balance would require a more complex set of built-in instructions than the competent system we have.

The kidneys do more than clean the blood. They also regulate the volume of blood by holding back fluid when fluid intake is low and by increasing urine output when fluid intake is high. When you drink a lot, you excrete a lot. Kidneys help regulate blood pressure. One symptom of kidney failure is soaring blood pressure. Kidneys also help the blood keep the right level of oxygen-carrying red cells. When a person is bleeding, the kidneys sense the lowered level of oxygen and signal the bone marrow to make more red blood cells.

With two kidneys, we have a backup system. If one kidney malfunctions, the healthy one enlarges a bit, becomes more efficient, and handles the whole work load. But kidneys are so crucial to life that the failure of both means certain death. It's no wonder, then, that so much research has centered on repairing diseased and damaged kidneys. Long before anyone transplanted a kidney, scientists experimented with ways to use an outside filter, a kind of artificial kidney that might take over long enough to give a damaged kidney time to heal.

The first experiment to show that an artificial kidney would be feasible took place in 1913 at Johns Hopkins University. A dog was given large doses of aspirin, and then its blood was filtered through a network of collodian tubes submerged in a liquid bath. To keep the blood from clotting, the heads of thousands of leeches were ground up and added because leeches were known to secrete an anticlotting substance. When the dog's blood went through the tubes, the aspirin was filtered out, showing that an outside "kidney" would work. Many years went by before the same experiment could be conducted on humans, however, because the leech extract wasn't practical, nor could the collodian filter tubes be used. A human artificial kidney had to wait for better materials. One was a drug called heparin, which keeps the blood from clotting, and the other was cellophane. The heparin was discovered and purified at Johns Hopkins in 1930. Cellophane had been invented by a French chemist in 1908, and it was used mainly for sausage casings.

Dr. Willem Kolff, who is director of the University of Utah's Division of Artificial Organs and is most famous for his work on the artificial heart, was practicing medicine in the Netherlands during World War II when the Nazis invaded his homeland. Under orders to continue work at the hospital, he set up the first blood bank in Europe, which he says taught him a lot about handling blood and helped him with the artificial kidney. A professor of biochemistry showed Dr. Kolff the wonders of cellophane, which was by then a cheap and common material that could be used to diffuse substances through its pores from one solution to another. Kolff took a section of cellophane sausage tubing and filled it with blood. He fastened this tubing on a small board and rocked it back and forth in a saline (saltwater) bath. When he added urea to the blood in the tube, Kolff found that in half an hour all the urea had passed out of the blood, through the cellophane, and into the saline solution. This kind of separation through a membrane is called dialysis.

All during the war, often working far into the night, Dr. Kolff built several of these dialysis machines or artificial kidneys. Finally he had one consisting of twenty yards of cellophane tubing wrapped

47

around a drum that rotated inside an enamel tank. An electric motor slowly turned the drum so that gravity would force the blood to flow through the tubing, submerged in the solution, and out the other end. But the equipment leaked at the connections where the blood entered and left the cylinder.

Dr. Kolff went to see the local Ford dealer because he knew that Henry Ford had made a tight seal around the water pump in his engines, and Kolff knew if that packing worked around a rotating joint well enough for an automobile, it ought to work in an artificial kidney. It did. Kolff tried his machine on fifteen patients before one recovered, but even those other comatose patients regained consciousness as their blood was cleaned. The year was 1946, and Kolff built eight extra artificial kidneys, using wood for the drums because of wartime shortages of metal. After the war when he found out that no one else had made an artificial kidney, he shipped the extra machines to hospitals in London, New York, and Montreal. Since then, of course, the machine has been refined and perfected.

Although the real kidney is complex, an artificial kidney is relatively simple. It uses the basic principle of diffusion of particles through a membrane. Dissolved molecules always move through a semipermeable membrane from an area of greater concentration to one of lesser concentration. During dialysis, blood flows from the patient's arm through a plastic tube into the dialysis machine, where it goes through cellophane cylinders awash in a fluid called the dialyzer. Cellophane is the semipermeable membrane. Its pores are big enough to let everything flow through except the blood cells and some of the larger proteins. The greater concentration of toxic wastes and water in the blood passes through the membrane into the solution. The "cleaned" blood continues on its way back to another vein in the patient's arm.

It doesn't hurt to be on a kidney machine. Most patients actually feel better as the toxic substances are filtered out of their blood.

Dr. Willem J. Kolff, inventor of the artificial kidney, at work in his laboratory at the University of Utah, where he is director of the Institute for Biomedical Engineering and the Division of Artificial Organs.   *(University of Utah)*

But neither is dependency on a machine an ideal way of life. Dialysis has many drawbacks. A wearable artificial kidney, called the WAK, was developed at the University of Utah, but that, too, is large and clumsy to use. Even with today's technology for miniaturizing systems, an artificial kidney that could take the place of two million nephrons would be too big to implant in a human body. There is no kidney as good as the real thing.

A kidney transplant requires only three connections: the artery supplying blood to the kidney, the vein taking blood away, and the ureter, which is the tube that drains urine to the bladder. But it's not the surgical technique that presented the main problem. It was getting the donor kidney to survive.

The first kidney transplant that can be called truly successful took place at Brigham Young Hospital in Utah in December 1954 when twenty-three-year-old Richard Herrick received a kidney from his identical twin brother. Transplants were not as successful for patients whose kidneys came from less perfectly matched donors. But since the development of better methods of tissue matching, the use of cyclosporine to control rejection, and federal funding for the costly surgery, there is only one major problem. There aren't enough kidneys available for all the people who need them.

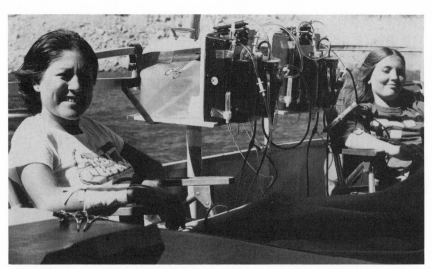

The WAK, or wearable artificial kidney, makes it unnecessary for patients to be hospitalized while they have their kidneys dialyzed or cleaned. These two young patients were able to relax aboard a houseboat on Lake Powell in southern Utah during treatment. *(University of Utah)*

If the kidney can be called the body's filter, the liver can be called the chemical factory. Made up of four lobes and weighing a little over three pounds, the liver lies alongside the stomach, just below the diaphragm. Along with the kidneys, the liver regulates the contents of the blood so that all the nutrients absorbed by the intestines after digestion are not dumped directly into the entire circulatory system.

The sugar glucose, for example, goes directly from the small intestine to the liver by way of the hepatic portal vein. Excess glucose is stored in the liver as glycogen. When the level of glucose in the blood falls, a condition called low blood sugar, the liver changes the stored glycogen back into glucose and sends it into the blood. A normal liver can store a twenty-four-hour supply of glucose as glycogen.

The liver changes some waste products into urea, which is removed by the kidneys, and it purifies toxic substances, making them inactive or at least less toxic. The liver also makes and releases into the bloodstream many blood proteins such as the blood-clotting proteins fibrinogen and prothrombin. Bile, which breaks down particles of fat for easier digestion, is made in the liver. The fat-soluble vitamins, A, D, E, and K, are stored in the liver. The amazing liver-factory also destroys old red blood cells and releases the iron in them to be used again.

Severe liver damage shuts down the factory. There are so many biochemical adjustments made in the liver that the body can't survive long without this truly vital organ. Fortunately, the liver is riddled with an enormous supply of blood vessels, which helps it heal and even regenerate to a limited degree. If up to one third of the liver is removed surgically, the remaining cells will reproduce until the liver is once again its normal size. But a liver destroyed beyond repair by cancer or other diseases also destroys the body unless it's replaced.

No one has made an artificial liver, and it's not likely anyone will try because it can't be a simple pump like the artificial heart, or just a filter like the artificial kidney. It would have to be an intricate factory. Fortunately, liver transplants work, with drugs to overcome rejection. If only there were enough organ donations to fill the need!

Transplant coordinators say that only one in one hundred deaths produces a liver for transplant, and most of those can be used only in adults because they are too large to fit in children. Unfortunately, the greatest need is among small children. In 1986 at the University of Chicago Medical Center, doctors placed a portion of an adult donor liver into a three-year-old child because the child's abdominal cavity was too small to hold the entire organ and because a child's liver was not available. If this is successful, one liver from a donor might be used in two transplants. It may even be possible to take a portion of a liver from a living donor, who could regenerate the missing portion, and that would be a perfect solution.

7

Thin
Skin

One sunny afternoon in July 1983 in Casper, Wyoming, five-year-old Jamie Selby, his six-year-old brother Glen, and a six-year-old friend were playing with paint. As they used paint remover to clean off paint they had splashed on one another, someone lit a match. The explosive fire killed the neighbor child and burned both Jamie and Glen over 97 percent of their bodies. Only the skin in their armpits and on small portions of their lower abdomens was unburned, but it was enough to save them because of a new way to grow "test-tube" skin from those few undamaged cells.

The skin is the largest organ in the human body. An organ is defined as a group of tissues joined structurally and cooperating functionally to perform a specific task. The skin qualifies. The pound and a half of different tissues that make up the skin stretches over twenty square feet, more or less, in a cooperative effort to keep us neatly together.

Our "birthday suit" is exactly that, a life-supporting space suit. It is a container and a shield against infection and ultraviolet light. It also plays a role in water balance, excretion, and the metabolism of vitamin D.

The skin varies from a thickness of $\frac{1}{25}$ of an inch over the eyelids to $\frac{3}{25}$ of an inch on the soles of the feet, but the top layer, called the epidermis, is a delicate $\frac{1}{250}$ of an inch thick. Epidermis is made up of squamous cells that start out plump and round at the bottom of this layer, but as they move upward during their fifteen- to thirty-day life, they flatten and die. Their protein turns into a tough, fibrous version called keratin, and the dead cells flake off as they get to the surface. It is this scalelike layer of dead cells that peels off after a sunburn. If it were not for the scaly cells falling off us like head-to-toe dandruff, we'd be half an inch thicker in a year's time.

The lower thick, spongy layer of skin, called the dermis, is mostly connective tissue that protects and cushions the body. Rich in the protein called collagen, this layer is packed with sweat glands and pores, hair follicles, blood vessels, oil glands, and the nerve endings that send and receive messages about touch, temperature, and pain. Beneath that is a layer of loose connective tissue and fat cells that binds the skin to the body and determines how much movement the skin will have.

Epithelial cells line or cover all the free body surfaces, both inside and out. In a dense, tightly packed layer, these epithelial cells build a continuous barrier to protect the lining of the digestive tract, the lungs, the blood vessels, the ducts and body cavities, as well as the outer portion of the skin.

Skin is also a habitat loaded with a teeming variety of bacteria and other microbes. Even clean skin is home to as much microscopic life as a sample of fertile soil, although the species of microbes are different. Arms, legs, and other patches of exposed skin are like deserts compared to the microbes found on protected skin.

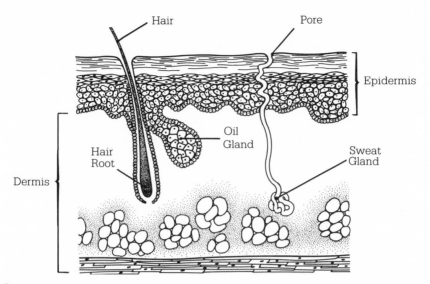

Cross section of the layers of skin

As long as the skin is undamaged, we're safe. But once the skin is broken, cut, or burned, we are open to attack from this horde of microbes.

Compared to other organs, skin is a simple structure, but it works in mysterious ways. Not only can it renew itself, but it can also recognize top from bottom as its epithelial cells push only in one direction. After years of research, several varieties of artificial skin have been made that can keep bacteria out and fluids in, but not one can assemble itself quite like the real thing.

Small sections of skin can be patched and stitched quite easily. They heal quickly. But when huge areas of skin are destroyed, life oozes away. There is no suffering to compare with that of a burn victim. A hospital burn unit has been called the closest thing to hell on earth because of the incredible agony suffered by burn patients. With skin stripped away, with no barrier to keep infection out or fluids in, the patient dehydrates and goes into shock.

Sunburn and other mild burns affect only the epidermis, and

this outer layer heals quickly. But if a large section of the lower layer of the dermis is destroyed, the cells no longer grow and move upward to the surface. These are the third-degree burns, which must be covered immediately. Even with instant attention, these are the burns that cause unbearable pain.

When the Selby boys arrived at Children's Hospital in Denver, their burns were cleaned and covered temporarily, but it was obvious that they would need extensive skin grafts. The best covering for a burn is an autograft, which is the patient's own skin taken from unburned portions of his body. Neither Jamie nor Glen Selby had enough skin for autografting.

Another choice is an allograft, or donor skin recovered from cadavers, but it is in short supply, and it can be rejected by the recipient. The most common burn coverings are heterografts, using the skin from animals, usually pigs, or artificial skin that is a combination of plastic and fibers from either sharks or cowhide. Both of these are temporary and must be removed or eventually covered with a layer of natural skin.

In a last great effort to save the boys, the doctors took a chance on a new technique that was still considered experimental. The Selby boys were flown to the Shriners' Burn Institute in Boston, where Dr. G. Gregory Gallico III and Dr. Howard Green, from Harvard Medical School, had developed a technique for making "test-tube" skin. Dr. Gallico took postage-stamp-size patches of skin from the boys' unburned underarms and lower abdomens. These bits of skin were minced and mixed in flasks with an enzyme that separated them into millions of individual cells, and some growth stimulants were added. During the twenty days it took for the cells to multiply in the flasks, the boys' burns were kept covered with temporary cadaver skin grafts and various artificial membranes. When the test-tube skin patches had grown to the size of playing cards, the temporary coverings were removed from boys' wounds. Each patch of newly grown skin was covered with Vaseline-coated gauze and laid, gauze side up, over the burns. When the gauze was peeled off a week later, the new skin was healthy and growing.

Jamie and Glen now have new skin, but it is shiny and smooth, without sweat glands or hair follicles. The boys may need more plastic surgery and therapy, but they have the protection of a skin that won't be rejected because it has grown from their own cells.

"Test-tube" skin is still experimental, and it is not the perfect treatment for all burn victims. One problem is the three-week delay in growing a large enough piece of skin for the transfer. In that time a burn patient can suffer complications and die.

Some researchers think that a thin covering, like the skin put on the Selby children, will not be strong enough. Dr. Ioannis Yannas, a professor of polymer science at Massachusetts Institute of Technology, and Dr. John F. Burke, a surgeon at Massachusetts General Hospital, have created a complex two-stage artificial skin. Dr. Yannas calls it the hundred-minute procedure. Within one hundred minutes from the time the burn victim enters the hospital, the graft has begun to work. A patch of skin the size of a quarter is taken from an unburned area of the patient, and the cells are centrifuged (spun around) to drive the youngest cells into a membrane. This cell-packed membrane is bandaged to the patient's burn wound, and within two weeks a new skin, called the neodermis, has begun to grow. Dr. Yannas says that while other groups wait two or three weeks for skin to grow in a flask, he puts the patient to work growing his own. The procedure is still experimental. The new skin will have no hair follicles or sweat glands, but it will be a living, growing skin.

Another lab is growing donor skin in large enough quantities to store in skin banks, where it will be immediately available to burn victims. Because the major problem with donor skin is rejection, a lot of work has gone into figuring a way around that. Dr. John Hefton, an immunologist at New York Hospital–Cornell

Dr. Ioannis Yannas with a piece of the artificial skin he developed at the Massachusetts Institute of Technology.   *(MIT photo by Calvin Campbell)*

Medical Center, has used an enzyme to remove one kind of skin cell that triggers the immune system to reject a foreign skin graft. So far the research shows that antigens, which warn the body about foreign invaders, can be lost when cells are cultured or grown under certain conditions in the lab. Skin twenty cell-layers thick has been grown by this experimental process and grafted with minimum scarring over large burned areas without rejection.

The goal is to come up with some kind of skin equivalent,

artificial or real, that can be stored frozen, ready for any emergency. It is no simple matter. A graft with skin stiffer than normal skin separates from the wound. In addition, the skin must be flexible enough to drape over all the different surfaces of the body—inside the armpit, under the knee, outside the elbow, or over a shoulder. Any kind of biomaterial must make close enough contact so pockets of air won't build up and open the wound to infection. It must be as resistant to moisture as the real thing. If too much water escapes, the patch will dry out, curl up, and separate. But it has to allow moisture to pass through to prevent fluid from building up. "Designer" skin has to be practical. It must be packaged for easy use and storage and be strong enough for handling and suturing during surgery. It should not alert the immune system, and it must be biodegradable so it can dwindle away at about the same rate as the new tissue that grows on the wound.

Many researchers think that if some kind of skin substitute can be built, it ought to be possible to make other kinds of organs as well. They've found that if they use patterns or templates of the organ, they can induce tissue to build a duplicate. Artificial blood vessels, an artificial thyroid gland, and cultured corneas are "on the bench" now. One of the most successful is a blood vessel made by using a plastic tube as the mold or shaping device. The tube is implanted under the skin of a sheep, which bothers the sheep not at all. While the animal wanders around the field and grazes, its body deposits a layer of the protein collagen around the shaping device. It's the same response a body has to any foreign object under the skin; it's a cover-up or walling off, an encapsulation. If a Y-shaped artery is desired, then a Y-shaped tube is inserted under the skin flap and sewn up. The finished tissue is strong and flexible enough to handle twice the pressure likely to be needed by the blood system.

Some thyroid gland equivalents have been cultured in rats using thyroid cells rather than epithelial cells, which are used for skin.

The thin tissue from a culture of the thyroid cells is implanted under a rat's skin. As blood vessels penetrate the tissue and nourish it, new thyroid cells gather. Rats who had had their thyroid glands removed gained weight when the artificially made thyroid equivalent was implanted. That meant the hormone thyroglobulin, which is made by the thyroid and is important in weight regulation, had passed into the bloodstream. In other words, the artificial thyroid worked.

One research team is trying to make a pancreas equivalent from tissue cultures of the beta cells that produce insulin. If it works, it will be an important step in the control of diabetes.

From there, it's only a matter of time before more complex organs are duplicated. But for now, the success of skin growth on people like Jamie and Glen Selby is miracle enough.

8

To Hear Again, Speak Again

Forty-three-year-old Craig Carpenter had been losing his hearing since he was three, and he'd been totally deaf for six years when he had an ear implant. He'd been told not to expect too much from the experimental implant, that perhaps he'd hear only the loudest noises, like a jet streaking overhead or horns honking in the street. But when he left the hospital, he heard the wind through the trees and the click of a camera.

In an interview he told a reporter, "All I really expected was that I could tell someone was trying to call my attention. But I'm hearing probably everything that's coming at me. I've not been able to identify everything yet."

Carpenter was the ninth person in the world to receive an extra-cochlear implant, which is a bioelectronic ear designed for deaf people who cannot be helped by hearing aids. It is not a cure, but it helps people whose deafness has been caused by disease or injury destroying some of the sensitive hair cells in the inner ear.

Sound energy travels through the air in waves, and when the waves strike an object, they cause the object to move or vibrate. When sound waves enter the ear, they pass through the outer to the middle ear, where they cause the eardrum and then three tiny bones to vibrate. The small bones pass along the vibrations to the snail-shaped organ of the inner ear, called the cochlea. The canals of the cochlea are filled with fluid and tiny hairlike cells. Hair cells convert the vibrations into electrochemical impulses that travel along the auditory nerve to the brain.

If the hair cells are destroyed, the connection is broken and the message or "sound" can't get through to the brain. It's like a telephone with no microphone. No amount of shouting at the wires will be heard through the system. Even if all other parts of the system work well, the sound can't get through. The usual hearing aid amplifies sound only to the outer ear, so it's no help to people with a broken connection to the nerve. An electronic cochlear implant bridges that gap. It takes over for the hair cells and stimulates the auditory nerve with electrical signals the brain interprets as sound.

Dr. William F. House, of the House Ear Institute in Los Angeles, developed one of the first cochlear implants in the 1960s, but his design didn't become really practical until advances were made in microsurgery, microelectronics, and implantable materials. A group of researchers at 3M adapted the House design. A tiny microphone, which can be clipped on eyeglasses or to clothing, picks up the sound and converts it to electrical impulses in a signal processor. The processor, which is no bigger than a deck of cards, can be carried in a pocket or clipped to a belt. It changes the electrical impulses from the microphone into magnetic signals, which can cross the skin without being felt. The impulses are carried through a thin cable to an external transmitter worn above and behind the ear. The transmitter is about the size of two stacked nickels, and it is held in place by magnetic attraction to the receiver implanted

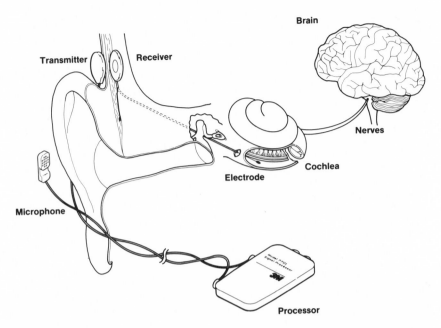

Outside the body, the user wears a tiny microphone with a small processor and a transmitter. The processor amplifies the electrical energy from the microphone, filters it, and sends it to the transmitter. The transmitter changes the electricity into magnetic signals so that no wires need pass through the skin. Magnetic currents cross the skin to the receiver without being felt. From the receiver, the signal travels to the cochlea by way of a wire electrode. Current flows between this electrode and a nearby ground electrode to stimulate the nerve fibers. The brain interprets this stimulation as sound.   *(3M)*

just under the skin. From the receiver, the signals go into the inner ear through the wire electrode, where they stimulate the nerve fibers, and the brain gets the message of sound.

Presently, the only people who can benefit from a cochlear implant are those who have postlingual deafness. That means they were able to hear at one time; they have some memory of sound and won't have to learn what sounds mean.

The sound isn't perfect. Not every user hears as well as Mr. Carpenter does with his implant. For some, the spoken words come through about like a radio that's not quite tuned in. Some users complain of hearing unwanted noises from power lines, two-way

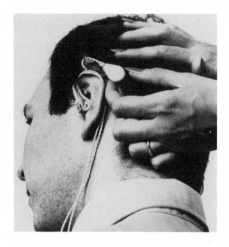

The external transmitter of the cochlear implant is held securely behind the ear by means of magnetic attraction to the implanted receiver. The sound signal passes from the transmitter across the skin to the receiver. *(3M)*

radios, refrigerator motors, light dimmers, and other sources of electrical energy. They even pick up interference from library and airport metal detectors.

Dr. Irwin A. Ginsburg, of Buffalo, New York, who implanted the cochlear device in Mr. Carpenter's ear, compares today's implants to the first crystal radio sets. The implants are in their infancy, but they will become more complex and effective as they are perfected.

While some learn to cope with the ordeal of hearing loss, others fight the frustration of not being able to speak. Every year in the United States, more than 20,000 people are afflicted with cancer of the larynx, and perhaps half of them lose their speech.

The larynx, or voice box, is a boxlike structure in the throat that serves as a passageway for air between the pharynx and the trachea. The ligaments of the larynx, called the vocal cords, are separated during breathing, but when we talk, the ligaments draw together and vibrate. The degree of tension on the cords changes the pitch, like strings on a guitar. Low notes come from relaxed cords; high pitch from the vibration of more tightly drawn cords. The sound is made by the vibration of the cords, but the words are made by the way we use the tongue, lips, palate, and teeth.

A laryngectomy is an operation that removes the larynx, and in order to keep an air passage open, a permanent opening called a tracheostoma is made through the patient's neck to the trachea. Without vocal cords, there is no voice, but several devices and methods have allowed these patients to talk again.

The first mechanism to produce artificial sound was a bellows device made in 1791 in Vienna by Wolfgang von Kempelerr. In the mid-1800s, when inventor Alexander Graham Bell and his brother were children, they rebuilt the bellows device to produce several intelligible sentences with it. They had grown up in a family interested in speech problems. Both their father and grandfather had studied the mechanics of sound and pioneered teaching speech to the deaf.

It wasn't until 1873 that the first artificial larynx was placed in a patient who had had a laryngectomy. Drawings and reports show that it must have been a clumsy, uncomfortable device, but it did produce a monotone that could be heard in a large hospital room. Of all the methods of helping a voiceless person speak, the earliest success came with what might be called the "gulp and burp" method. The patient literally gulps and swallows air to burp up as he forms the words. It's not easy. There's no way to control volume, or to make the words clear, or to carry on a long conversation without tiring.

There is a battery-powered device called an electrolarynx that produces sound when it's held against the neck. Low-frequency vibrations create sound in the pharynx, which can become speech as the person mouths the words. Another sound source is made by an electronic vibrating device that enters the mouth through a tube placed between the lips. When it is turned on, a low-pitched sound enters the mouth, and the user forms words with the tongue, palate, and teeth. The "voice" from these devices is a mechanical, monotonous sound, and the speaker has to hold the gadget in his hand, which makes it difficult to do anything else at the same time.

The newest artificial larynx is built into an appliance that fits in the mouth like a dental bridge or a retainer. It can even be built into an upper denture plate. It can't be seen, and it leaves the hands free because it is turned on and off with a touch of the tongue. Two small three-volt batteries power a speaker system that produces a humming tone in the mouth. Talking in the usual way with lips and tongue turns these humming tones into a voice.

Two other devices, one called a "voice button" and the other called a "duckbill," do not use an electronic vibrator. They consist of small tubelike valves inserted in an opening made by a surgeon between the patient's trachea and esophagus. The tubes are one-way valves that keep food and fluids from leaking out of the esophagus into the trachea, but allow air to go from the trachea into the esophagus. When the opening, the tracheostoma, is covered with the thumb or finger, air from the lungs is forced from the trachea into the esophagus. The esophagus vibrates with a low-pitched sound that can be turned into words.

Computers have come to the aid of thousands of people who can't speak easily or clearly. Scott is a bright five-year-old who can read and write, but the sounds he makes for speech aren't clear enough to be understood. A birth injury cost him control of the face muscles and the use of a normal palate. Now he has a "Touch Talker" computer programmed with a language called "Minispeak" that works with symbols and letters. On the 128 keys, Scott can touch any number of combinations to have as big a vocabulary as anyone he knows, if not bigger.

Retired nurse Myrtice Fuller, of Hyannis, Massachusetts, can't use her fingers to press the keys of a computer. An Associated Press news story told how she can "speak" with the flick of an eyebrow. Miss Fuller suffers from amyotrophic lateral sclerosis, more commonly known as Lou Gehrig's disease after the famous baseball player afflicted by this neurological disorder. It causes gradual paralysis. She wears a headband with a small electronic switch just above one eyebrow. When she wants to talk, she watches a TV screen where a cursor moves over a list of letters. With incredible patience, Miss Fuller waits for the cursor to land on the letter she wants. If she moves her eyebrow a beat too soon or too late, she has to wait for the cursor's next sweep across the letters. Her computer has been programmed with a list of commonly used words and phrases so that she may ask for an extra pillow or a drink of water with the flick of an eyebrow. Computers can be adapted to switch on with the slightest pressure exerted by almost anything—a thumb, a pillow, a foot, a chin, or a wand held in the teeth.

Miss Fuller can choose to have her words printed out or spoken by the voice synthesizer, which has a robotlike male voice. But even that has been improved upon. Newer computer programs can more nearly imitate the user's voice. A child sounds like a child, an older woman like an older woman. At a conference on the handicapped recently, one computer group demonstrated a "workless station," an optical character reader that converts some printed type directly to a disk, eliminating the need to key in anything. This will work with a machine called DECTALK that converts text to speech. Anything that appears on the screen can be said in a choice of eight voices or a customized blend. It even sings!

9

The Plastic Window

Two ideas that stuck in the mind of British eye surgeon Dr. Harold Ridley have resulted in better vision for millions of people whose eyes were clouded by cataracts. The first idea came from a young medical student who was in the operating room watching Dr. Ridley remove a cataract from a patient, and the second idea was triggered by a World War II fighter plane.

Light passes through the lens of the eye just as it does through the lens of a camera. A cataract is a clouding of this usually clear lens. It is not a film over the eye or an infection or a growth, but the result of chemical changes inside this pea-sized lens. It is a normal part of aging. If we live long enough, almost all of us will develop cataracts. Sometimes children are born with cataracts or develop them through disease, but those cases are not common. For more than 3,000 years we've been aware of cataracts, and the name comes from an Arabic word meaning "black water." During the Middle Ages this description of "black water" was translated into Latin as a waterfall or *cataracta,* which then became cataract.

There is no medicine to stop or reverse the development of a cataract, and the standard treatment is the removal of the clouded lens. The National Society to Prevent Blindness estimates that a million such surgeries took place in 1984. Once the cataract is removed, it cannot return. But in order to see again, the patient must have some kind of replacement lens. For many years, the only choice was inch-thick "Coke bottle" glasses. Not only did these cumbersome lenses make the wearer's eyes look enormous, but they were difficult to adjust to. Everything looks 25 percent larger through these huge lenses. If only one cataract is removed and a thick lens is worn over just one eye, the brain gets an image 25 percent bigger from the corrected eye. That causes distortion and confusing double vision. Seen through thick cataract glasses, a doorway looks barrel-shaped instead of rectangular.

When contact lenses were invented, many of these problems were solved, but not all of them. Tiny contact lenses are difficult for some elderly people with shaky hands to handle. They are easy to lose and hard to find, especially when vision isn't good to begin with, and contacts can't always be tolerated for long periods of time.

When Dr. Ridley put his two ideas together, he solved some of these problems with a permanent implantable lens. The medical student who had watched Dr. Ridley remove a cataract from a patient asked the surgeon if he had forgotten to replace the cloudy lens with a new clear one. Never having seen such surgery before, the student assumed that would be the next step. Dr. Ridley couldn't get that idea out of his mind; it seemed such a sensible solution. He may even have remembered that the technique had been tried in 1795 when an Italian surgeon, Casaamata, put a tiny crystal lens into a man's eye. The lens, unfortunately, didn't work because it dropped to the bottom of the eye, where it couldn't help the patient's vision.

As he began to think about what kind of artificial lens the eye would tolerate, Dr. Ridley remembered that during World War II he had treated pilots whose planes had been hit by enemy fire. The cockpit of the British Spitfire fighter plane was covered with a plastic canopy, and when that canopy shattered, splinters of plastic were often embedded in the pilots' eyes. The usual treatment was to leave the splinters untouched because surgeons were afraid of injuring the eye even more. Then an interesting thing happened. The eyes healed around the splinters without infection. Ridley decided that this plastic, called polymethylmethacrylate (PMMA), which was so well tolerated by the eye, would be the perfect material for an artificial lens.

On November 29, 1949, at the St. Thomas Hospital in London, Dr. Ridley implanted an artificial plastic lens into the eye of a forty-five-year-old woman. Even though several implants were successful, Ridley stopped performing the operations in 1960 because he found that, in too many cases, the lens dropped to the floor of the eye as the crystal lens had in the 1795 surgery.

Several other surgeons kept working on ways to insert the implant so it wouldn't move, and today 75 percent of all cataracts are corrected by implants called intraocular lenses (IOL). Made of the same PMMA plastic that was used in the Spitfire canopies, the IOL fits behind the iris with tiny flexible "arms" called haptics to hold it in place. The IOL is limited to a 1 percent magnification, which allows cataract patients the most normal vision possible today.

During surgery, which is often performed with the patient under local anesthetic, the surgeon removes the cloudy cortex of the lens. Before the plastic lens is implanted, the surgeon checks it carefully under the microscope to make sure it is perfect because it has to stay in the eye for the patient's lifetime. As the IOL is slipped into place, the surgeon must be careful not to let any of the eye's aqueous fluid leak out because that might cause the cornea to collapse against the implant. A clear jellylike, gluey substance called

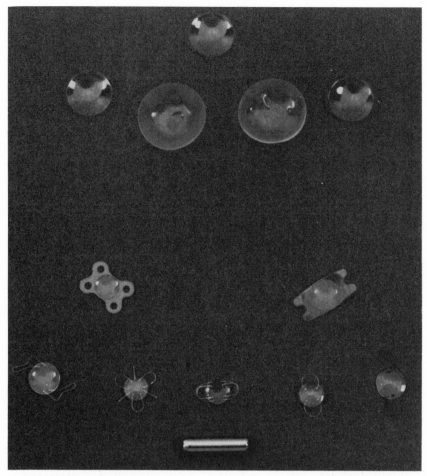

Contact lenses, shown on the top row, and implantable intraocular lenses, shown below, must be made of material that will not scratch or irritate the eyes. These various designs went through rigorous testing in the surface science laboratories of the Calspan Corporation. *(Calspan Corporation)*

Healon, made from the combs of roosters, can be injected into the eye as a cushion to support the cornea. Originally, Healon was used as a shock absorber in the knees of racehorses.

Although the IOL is an incredible spare part for the eye, it can't repair damage done by chemical burns, bacterial infections, or a

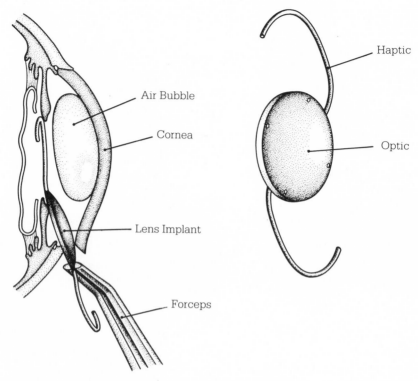

This diagram shows how an artificial lens is implanted. An air bubble has been injected into the eye to keep the cornea from collapsing against the lens.

penetrating injury from a pointed stick or a knife. When the clear, tough dime-size cornea, which covers the eye like the crystal over a watch, is damaged, the only thing that will fix it is a new cornea.

Sister Mary Yvonne Moran is one of thousands who can see through the eyes of another person. On the day after Christmas 1948, in a small town in Mississippi, the young nun was watching some children celebrate by tossing "torpedoes." "They were small firecrackers shaped like silver balls," she remembers. "I was quite daring in those days, and I asked if I could try one. It exploded in my face. I was glad afterward that I had lighted that one; otherwise, one of those boys would have taken the impact of the explosion."

Bits of paper and powder from the firecracker were embedded in one of Sister Yvonne's corneas, but all the doctor could do for her was clean it and watch for infection. He told her that scar tissue would mar her cornea, but there would be worse scarring if he tried to remove the debris. As the years went by, that eye grew cloudy from a cataract as well. It wasn't until 1983 that Sister Yvonne heard about corneal transplants. Her eye rejected the first donor cornea, but two years later she received another. And now she can see.

Rejection is much less a problem in corneal transplants than in any other because the cornea has no blood supply. There is no tissue matching, and almost anyone can be a donor. Although the corneas must be taken from the donor within hours after death, they can be kept in good condition for four days before they are transplanted.

When a donor cornea becomes available, the doctor calls the patient, and surgery is scheduled as soon as possible. Advances in surgical techniques and equipment have made this such a safe operation that it is usually performed with the patient under local

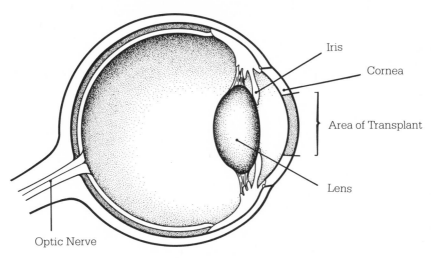

Cross section of the eye showing the position of the cornea transplant

anesthetic. Corneas originally were removed from the donor's eye in a rectangular sheet and then shaped to the recipient's eye. Now the cornea is cut from the donor with a gadget like a high-tech cookie cutter. The same instrument is used to cut out the exact size opening in the patient's cornea. The donor cornea is lifted into the patient's eye by two nylon threads and stitched in place with thread half the thickness of a human hair. Working under a surgical microscope, the surgeon can zoom in and see the eye magnified forty times. Most surgeons cover the transplanted cornea with a contact-lens bandage to keep the loose ends of the stitches from irritating the eyelid. There is no pain, and the patient can go home shortly after the transplant.

After a month or two the first stitch is removed, and in order to prevent strain on the healing cornea, the other stitches are taken out one at a time over the next six months. Healing is slow because the cornea is nourished by the aqueous humor and other tissues of the eye, rather than by a direct blood supply.

In 1985, banks across the country that were members of the Eye Bank Association of America distributed 20,250 corneas for the most common of all the transplant procedures. Most recipients have their vision restored to 20/40, and a substantial number of people return to normal 20/20 vision with the use of glasses.

The corneal transplants work wonders for people blinded by clouded corneas, but when blindness originates in the retina, there is little that can be done. Like a curved movie screen covering the inner surface of the eye, the retina receives light coming into the eye. Actually an extension of the brain itself, the retina is a complex layer of neurons including the light-sensitive rods and cones that allow us to see in color or black and white. At the University of Rochester, New York, a group of scientists has been successful in transplanting retinal cells from embryo rats into the retinas of rats whose blindness was caused by viruses or chemicals. The blind rats did not suddenly see again, but the microscopic patches of retinal cells did grow in the host eye, and that is miraculous enough for this first step. It means that the process is possible. "The difficulties are many and the goal distant," says a report from the University of Rochester. But scientists know that if further experiments are successful, it will be a giant step toward curing one of the most dreaded of human physical problems.

10

The Gift
of Life

How do you ask a man for his son's heart?

Where do you find a healthy liver that could save a child's life?

It's not easy. Not a day goes by without the chance for one person's tragedy to turn into another person's miracle.

John was an eighteen-year-old high school senior riding home from football practice one August night when a car sideswiped his motorcycle, leaving him "brain-dead." His EEG (electroencephalogram) recorded no brain waves, nor was there a single response to any of the other standard and absolutely decisive tests for life, even while John's heart and lungs were kept working on a respirator.

Several months before the accident, John and his family had watched a television program about transplants, and they had talked about organ donation. In midst of their shock and grief over their son's death, John's parents didn't want to think about anyone else's problems. But they remembered that John had thought organ donation was a great idea, and they gave the hospital permission to use his healthy organs. Within hours, John's heart was on its way to a thirty-nine-year-old father of four. One kidney was given to a young science teacher, and the other was transplanted into a seventeen-year-old waitress who had been surviving on kidney dialysis for four years. John's liver was transplanted into a nineteen-year-old college student, and two other people were able to see again with the corneas from John's eyes.

Each year some 23,000 people are involved in accidents that leave them brain-dead, but fewer than 3,000 of those tragedies result in organ donations. Surgical teams at organ transplantation centers are ready around the clock, every day of the year, to recover organs and transplant them. Why, then, are so few organs used?

"Can you imagine how difficult it is to go to the parents of a dying child and ask them to sign a legal paper giving away parts of that child to someone they don't even know?" one emergency room nurse asked. "Time is crucial. It has to be done immediately. And yet you have to convince them that the doctors and nurses have done everything in their power to keep their child alive. I understand how they feel. They've just heard the worst news they'll ever get, and an outsider is suddenly asking them to think about the lives of others."

In many hospitals, a person called an organ procurement coordinator or a transplant coordinator is responsible for asking the grieving families to donate organs and for matching them with those who need a specific organ. One coordinator, describing a typical situation, said, "On this job you run through all the emotions. It's very sad to ask for the donation, but when you follow it through and see how many people are helped, it's incredibly rewarding."

A coordinator at St. Luke's Medical Center in Chicago said that one morning she was called to the intensive care unit of a hospital because a fifteen-year-old boy had been declared clinically brain-dead. He had been riding his bicycle when he was hit by a car, leaving him with extensive and irreversible brain damage. Although his parents were overcome with grief, they knew they did not want their son lingering on a respirator.

The boy was receiving oxygen from a ventilator that made his heart beat artificially. He could not breathe on his own, and he had no response to pain. Because in this situation the patient's chest is moving and his skin has good color and feels warm, it may be difficult to believe the patient is really dead. Off the respirator, however, a brain-dead person would not be able to breathe and his heart would stop. No patient who has met the stringent criteria of brain death has ever lived.

Brain death is not the same as a coma, in which a person's brain activity may be recorded. In total brain death, both the voluntary and involuntary responses stop working. Breathing is an involuntary function of the autonomic nervous system; you don't have to think about it. The voluntary nervous system controls conscious actions like muscular movement. In brain death, it's as though the main switch has been pulled.

The family of this boy faced three choices. They could keep their son on artificial life-support, but his body would quickly deteriorate and his heart soon would stop beating. They could choose to discontinue any life-support and simply wait for him to die. Or they could donate their son's organs for transplant while those organs were still being supplied with oxygen. The family chose to donate the organs because it was a way of turning a tragic death into a heroic event. Had they decided to allow their son to die slowly on the respirator, the organs in his body would have been useless.

Organs are *never* recovered from a body without the written consent of the family. Even if the patient had at some time signed a donor card or a "living will" indicating that he wanted to give his organs, the actual removal of the organs, in this country, does not take place without written permission. Next of kin who sign the consent form may even specify which organs may be taken. One family allowed all the organs to be used except their son's eyes. Requests of that kind are always honored.

In the case of the fifteen-year-old Chicago boy, the moment the parents signed the permission forms, the transplant coordinator put a well-rehearsed plan into action. First, she entered the weight, blood type, age, and sex of the donor into a telephone computer system called NATCO 24-Alert Organ Sharing System. The North American Transplant Coordinators Organization created this computer program in 1983 at the University of Pittsburgh in order to match donors and recipients at any time, anywhere, with one phone call. If the organs can't be used locally, they are sent out. In a few minutes, the computer screen displayed which transplant centers in North America had people who needed this boy's organs. The coordinator made the necessary phone calls to alert the transplant teams from those centers and to schedule an operating room. The recovery of organs is carried out under the same careful, sterile conditions used for any surgery.

The next step was ordered and disciplined. A highly trained surgical team of four from Yale University Hospital, scheduled to recover the liver, flew to Chicago where an ambulance met them for a fast ride to the hospital. A team of seven cardiac specialists from Loyola University in Chicago was flown by helicopter directly to the hospital grounds because every minute counts in recovering a heart. The team of seven surgeons from nearby Rush Medical Center drove to the hospital because the kidneys they would recover could be preserved longer than the other organs. Eye surgeons from the Illinois Eye Bank were scheduled last because the recovery of the corneas for transplant can be done after the patient is removed from the respirator. Corneas can be stored in a tissue bank for up to four days.

Like the producer of a stage show, the coordinator arranged every detail so that each team's time in the operating room went smoothly and transportation from airport to hospital and back was as fast as possible. Most recovery teams have to take the first available commercial flight, but in some areas corporations donate a jet and crew for the team's use. Timing is crucial, especially for the recovery of heart and liver, which are stored in a "slush" solution of ice and water. Kidneys, with a longer preservation time, are usually delivered in a regular picnic cooler.

While all the organizing is going on, the nurses in the intensive care unit keep the brain-dead patient's vital signs as stable as possible. With the respirator forcing oxygen into the lungs, the heart continues to pump the oxygenated blood to the organs, and the kidneys continue to get rid of the waste.

"We miss an awful lot of organ donations because someone doesn't want to ask," said Laureen Dunn, former director of the Organ Procurement Agency in Buffalo, New York. "In one year we were able to match donors and recipients for forty kidneys, six hearts, seven livers, and many corneas for the eye bank. But we have a constant list of seventy waiting for kidneys, and those are critical. There are more than 60,000 people on kidney dialysis in this country, and between 10,000 and 12,000 are potential candidates for transplant. Some don't want one. Some are too old or too ill. Many are small children, too young and in unstable condition.

"We have lots of livers," she said. "Most of them are needed by small children who have a disorder called biliary atresia. It's a total breakdown of the bile ducts in the liver. But the livers we often recover are from adults, and they are too large for children."

The American Council on Transplantation, formed in 1983, says that the shortage of donors is caused by people's not knowing about the need or being misinformed. They don't know how transplantation is done or how much it costs. The expense of transplantation is enormous, but it costs nothing to be a donor. A physician, who has since lost his license to practice medicine in several states, appeared on a national television talk show promoting his plan for going to Third World nations to buy kidneys. Some new laws will protect against that kind of exploitation. In 1981, Georgia was the only state to specifically forbid the sale of cadaver organs, but New York and other states have adopted similar laws since.

Because most patients who become donors arrive at the hospital in critical condition, permission must come from family members. Until 1986, there was no way to require hospital officials to ask for organ donations. In the first states to pass "required request" legislation, California, Oregon, New York, and Connecticut, hospitals reported enormous increases in the number of donations. Most transplant coordinators believe it won't be long before all states will require an organ donation request on hospital admission forms.

In Denmark, France, Switzerland, Austria, and some other countries, organs are retrieved from cadavers under the policy of "presumed consent," unless the family objects. Finland, Greece, Norway, Spain, and Sweden also use the policy of presumed consent, although doctors do ask permission of the families as well. The policy of saving lives is given first priority in these countries. In all the English-speaking countries, nothing is presumed, and signed consent is essential. The Uniform Anatomical Gift Act, which legalizes organ donation, specifies who may sign the written permission: a spouse, adult son or daughter, either parent, adult brother or sister, a guardian of the person, or any other person authorized to care for the body at the time of death.

Why, then, sign a donor card and carry it in your wallet? The American Council on Transplantation suggests that anyone who signs a donor card should discuss the matter with family members because the card will serve as a reminder to them at the time of the person's death.

Some people sign living wills or trusts, which are simply state-

If death is imminent, please call Kidney Hotline (716) 883-0003

UNIFORM DONOR CARD

OF_____

Print or type name of donor

In the hope that I may help others, I hereby make this anatomical gift, if medically acceptable, to take effect upon my death. The words and marks below indicate my desires.

I give: (a) _____ any needed organs or parts

(b) _____ only the following organs or parts

_____

Specify the organ(s) or part(s)

for the purposes of transplantation, therapy, medical research or education;

(c) _____ my body for anatomical study if needed.

Limitations or
special wishes, if any :_____

08-21-79/100M

A Uniform Donor Card is a reminder to families that the signer wished to have his or her organs used by others. *(National Kidney Foundation)*

ments of intent filed with an attorney, usually declaring that they don't want their life extended by artificial means such as a respirator and that they want to donate their organs for transplantation.

There are those who do not participate in organ donation because their religion forbids it. The Orthodox Jewish religion, for example, does not allow burial of a disfigured or mutilated body in a consecrated cemetery, and the loss of an organ is considered a disfigurement.

But the need is great. Skin is a scarce resource, especially as a covering for burn victims. A layer only as thin as that peeled in sunburn is taken from a donor. Bones are used from donors between seventeen and fifty-five years of age. Under seventeen, the bones are not developed enough, and beyond fifty-five, diseases such as osteoporosis may have set in. The bones are used mainly for transplantation where there has been bone loss from injury or where tumors or infections have destroyed the bone. The donor bones are x-rayed, tagged, and stored in a freezer. When a surgeon

82

is looking for an exact bone size, it's easy to find it in the x-ray file. Most of the bone banks have been nothing more than small freezers, where one or two surgeons store bones for use only with their own patients, but larger commercial bone banks have been organized in some cities. One in St. Louis is run by the American Red Cross, and there are other large storage centers in Miami, San Francisco, and Portsmouth, Virginia.

In 1984, some 24,000 corneas were transplanted in the United States with a 90 percent success rate for the graft. There was an 80 percent success rate for the 346 heart transplants, and a 65 percent success rate with the 308 liver transplants. Of the 6,968 kidney donations, 96 percent were successful.

According to the National Heart Transplantation Study, there are 15,000 people who need hearts, 8,500 who are waiting for liver transplants, and 5,000 who would benefit from pancreas transplants. Organ transplants have become accepted procedures. Who wouldn't want a child or other family member to receive a transplant that might save his or her life or extend it for a few years while medicine searched for other solutions?

Transplant coordinators agree that most donor families have two things in common: generosity and sensitivity. They want to make something good come out of tragedy.

11

Designer Bones

A quarterback snatches the ball, pivots to the right, and falls to the ground in agony. He wasn't hit by a tackle. His knee gave way. The human knee was not made for the sudden starts, stops, or quick twists of football. Nor was it built for the rigors of tennis, basketball, or ballet.

The average career in the National Football League lasts only 4.6 years because of knee injuries, which account for 25 percent of athletic injuries serious enough to sideline the players for at least a week. Seventy percent of professional football players have knee surgery before they are twenty-six years old. Knee injuries sideline the "weekend warriors," too, in tag football or city park soccer. Joggers and aerobic enthusiasts feel the agony of knee pain, which is not surprising when you know that even climbing stairs or getting up from a chair puts a load on the knee joint more than five times the person's body weight. The knee is the most injury-prone of all joints, and it's often called upon for more than it can deliver.

The joints in our fingers are simple hinges. The saddle joints of the spine allow us to sway from side to side, bend from front to back, and move in small arcs. The ball-and-socket joint of the hip can rotate. But the knee is more complex. It's a hinge that extends and flexes, but also moves from side to side, swivels, twists, slides, and glides. Ballet star Mikhail Baryshnikov could not leap high and land softly with a mere hingelike knee, nor could tennis pro Chris Evert rush to the net, pivot, and race to the baseline to retrieve a lob.

Knee injuries came with the territory when humans began walking upright. The knees of other mammals don't give way because they have the stability of four legs, and their feet don't effectively seal the bottom of the leg to the ground as ours do. With the extra adhesion of cleats or other special soles on sneakers, the feet of

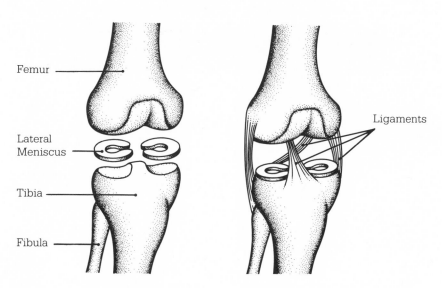

The knee has little protection. The lateral meniscus is one of the pads of cartilage that act as a shock absorber.

athletes tend to stay even more firmly planted when the upper body makes a quick twist.

The knee is made up of three bones: the femur or thighbone, the tibia or shinbone, and the patella or kneecap. C-shaped crescents of cartilage, called the menisci, are the shock absorbers that keep the femur and tibia from grinding against each other. Unlike the hip joint that is protected and surrounded by a mass of muscle, the knee is held together by four major ligaments. If those ligaments are torn, the knee not only becomes loose and wobbly, but the chances for developing arthritis and other degenerative joint diseases greatly increase.

Bone is one of nature's strongest, toughest, most resilient composite materials. It's made up of minute crystals of a calcium mineral bonded with collagen fibers. The effect of these rigid particles held together with an elastic glue is incredible shock resistance. Bone is also porous, making it even better able to resist cracks from stress as it grows.

A layer of smooth, glossy microporous cartilage covers the surface of the joints. That cartilage is surrounded by a tough synovial membrane that secretes a transparent fluid that has the consistency of egg white. All the spaces of a joint are filled with this synovial fluid, which is absorbed by the microporous cartilage layer. Pressure points in any joint are changing constantly in a sliding, rolling action, and the synovial fluid keeps that area lubricated. When the pressure point changes, the synovial fluid is absorbed, ready for the next cycle.

It's a hard system to match, but we try. According to the Arthritis Foundation, each year there are some 150,000 joint replacements.

An artificial hip joint consists of a ten-inch metal spike inserted into the femur (thighbone), with a sphere on top that is the ball part of the ball-and-socket hip joint. The sphere, which must have a mirror finish in order to move smoothly, fits into a cup made of polyethylene. Some spikes and balls are made from stainless steel; others are titanium alloys or ceramics. All the materials must be biocompatible, lightweight, tough, and corrosive resistant. The newest acrylic bone cement anchors the spike into the femur with a material similar to that used by dentists to take impressions. It doesn't actually adhere to the bone. It holds because it is porous, allowing the bone to penetrate and anchor the replacement part.

An artificial knee is a last resort, and even then, a young person is almost never a candidate for one because an artificial joint doesn't last long enough. Sixty-year-old Edward Hannah, from Columbus, Ohio, whose x-ray is shown on page 88, can work and play golf more comfortably with the artificial joint than he could with an arthritis-crippled knee. Even the more protected hip replacements, which last about ten years, are reserved for older people who are less likely to give them zealous workouts.

The first metal knee and hip joints were difficult to fit with precision, and they loosened with wear. Many set off metal detectors in airports. Better designs were mass-produced in a wide variety of sizes a surgeon could order from the factory. But the newest joints are custom-designed and made by computer. The new "press-fit" knee fits almost like the real thing. Information about hundreds of normal knees is fed into a computer along with

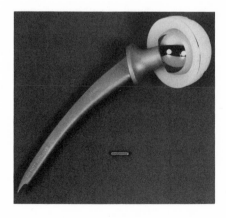

An artificial hip must be designed with a long shaft made of material that will grip and adhere securely in the femur, but with a ball joint that will move smoothly and freely in the hip socket. *(Calspan Corporation)*

measurements of the patient's height, build, and bone structure. The computer can predict just what this person's knee would have been like if it weren't arthritic or damaged. It simulates the motion paths and joint forces of bone, muscles, and ligaments. After the ideal knee is designed and "installed" on the computer screen, the data is sent to the factory, where a perfect knee is machine-tooled by computer.

The loss of one of our adult teeth leaves a gap in the jawbone. The bone in that space is gradually reabsorbed by the body. To fill in the gap with something more comfortable than a bridge or denture, an experimental artificial bone has been made from a mixture of fired ceramic particles of hydroxyapatite (the primary calcium compound in bone) and plaster of Paris, which is also a calcium compound. When the mixture is moistened into a claylike consistency, it can be molded into the repair site. The plaster works

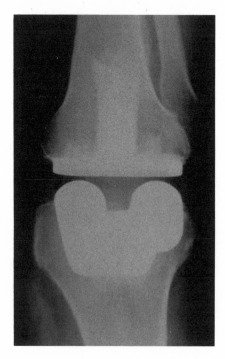

X-ray of one kind of artificial knee used to replace a knee damaged by arthritis. (Edward Hannah, Sr., and David K. Halley, M.D. [F.A.C.S.], Columbus, Ohio)

like a temporary scaffold to hold the particles in place while the new tissue grows. The plaster itself is gradually absorbed by the body. This new artificial bone material can also be used to patch holes in bone, to reshape bone during plastic surgery, and to mend fractures and spinal column defects.

False teeth have been a common spare part for centuries, but none can ever work as well or be as comfortable as a tooth anchored firmly in the jaw. One kind of permanent replacement puts fixtures that look like screws into the jaw and attaches artificial teeth to them. The screws are made of pure titanium because it bonds with human bone and provides a stable but invisible base for the teeth. This technique works equally well to implant an entire mouthful of teeth or a single tooth.

If you've ever had a broken arm or leg, you know it heals, but the actual fact is that bones do not heal themselves. Fractures knit because of new bone made from other tissue. The old bone no

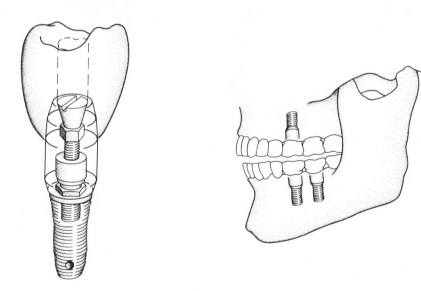

A screw made from pure titanium is implanted surgically into the jawbone, and three to six months after surgery, an artificial tooth can be installed on this permanent base.

longer has the capacity to grow. Two tissues make the new bone at the break site. One is the bone's fibrous covering called the periosteum; the innermost cells of this layer are somehow turned on when there is a fracture. The other healing tissue is the bone marrow, which goes through a sequence of cell changes that causes regrowth. Sometimes in a complex fracture, when metal plates, screws, and nails are used to hold the bone fragments together, the periosteum and the marrow are injured, and as a result healing is slowed. In addition, a metal plate prevents the bone from carrying the weight, and when it's removed, the bone is still fragile and easily broken again.

One research team uses a polymer clamp on broken bones because it is chemically absorbed by the body. Stiff enough to hold the broken bone in place until it heals, the clamp gradually degrades, allowing the broken bone to carry a normal load as it heals.

Although no one is certain exactly how or why it works, it's been found that broken bones often mend more quickly with electrical stimulation. This research originated in Japan in the 1950s, and three electrical stimulation bone-growth systems have been approved by the FDA for use in the United States. It's a field full of unknowns, but orthopedic surgeon Robert O. Becker believes the same factors that switch on the cells in a salamander's amputated leg to start regeneration are the ones involved in this regrowth of bone triggered by an electrical current.

The ideal solution to a lost limb would be, of course, to grow a new one. But until we learn how to do that, the next best solution is a man-made limb connected directly to the skeleton, where it can be hooked up to receive command information from the nerves. Such a limb can feed back to the brain information about the position of the limb as well as the weight and texture of the object it is touching. One designer of artificial limbs says that the limb and its controller must be thought of as one system.

Whether you climb on a stool to reach for a book on a high shelf or compete as a gymnast in the Olympic games, your muscles perform with precision. They are powerful, fast, smooth, silent, highly efficient, and almost impossible to copy. Try to pick up a cup and drink from it without turning your wrist. It can't be done. We take for granted the twenty-seven motions a human arm is capable of making. The best version of an artificial arm can make about six of these motions—a far cry from the natural arm. Since the 1950s there have been many attempts to build an arm that moves smoothly, and one of the newest is the Utah arm.

Alice Olson, from Westfir, Oregon, was the first amputee to be fitted with the only totally electric "elbow" and hand system in the world. Two electrodes on Ms. Olson's remnant muscles monitor electrical signals and send control information that operates the elbow and hand, which are used in combination with the Utah arm. With this system, it is not necessary to use the kinds of control cables that operate traditional artificial limbs. *(University of Utah)*

Developed at the University of Utah Medical Center, the Utah arm is a myoelectric system, which means that small signals measured in units of one millionth of a volt (microvolts) emitted by the muscles are amplified 300,000 times to activate controls. The sleeve of the artificial arm contains these electrodes. When the arm is put on, the electrodes pick up signals from the muscles and pass them to small motors that move the arm. Such a prosthesis can lift three pounds, and when it is locked, it can support loads up to fifty pounds. A cable-operated hook or a hand is attached to the arm at the wrist. It is sometimes difficult to tell the real thing from a Utah arm because it can swing freely, works silently and quickly, and matches the wearer's skin in color and texture.

When Jeff Mayer gets ready for his daily run, he takes off his walking shoes and puts on his running shoes. He also changes his feet. Since he lost both legs in Vietnam, he owns two pairs of feet, one for walking and the new Seattle one for running. At the Pros-

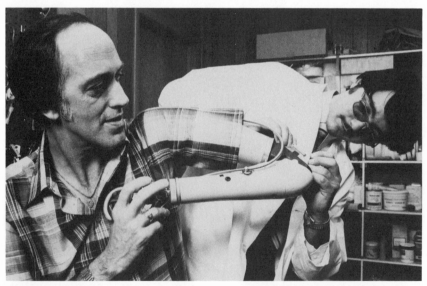

J. Thomas Andrew checks the miniaturized electronics that control the Utah arm worn by Larry Campbell of Roy, Utah. The arm, developed by Dr. Stephen C. Jacobsen, director of the University of Utah's Center for Biomedical Design, is controlled by the wearer's own muscles. *(University of Utah)*

thetics Research Study Center in Seattle, Washington, this artificial foot was made to bend and add a spring to the step as if foot muscles were lifting it, with the kind of stability a foot gets from its many small bones.

Jeff Keith, who lost a leg to cancer, helped raise money for cancer research by completing a 3,350-mile run across the United States wearing an artificial leg attached to a Seattle foot. In an interview

Jeff Keith ran 3,350 miles across the United States wearing an artificial leg as part of his campaign to help the American Cancer Society raise funds and to remind people that he, and others like him, are not physically handicapped, but physically challenged. *(American Cancer Society)*

93

on the Phil Donahue television show he said, "It gives you an actual spring toe action, so every time you walk, it fires forward for you. There is a lot of work being done in research, but people need to be aware that there are legs out there that are better than they have. I can run a nine-minute mile.

"I consider myself physically challenged. We want to promote the message that any restriction that confronts one person can really be overcome with hard work and determination."

Jeff Keith shared time on that television program with Nan Davis, who overcame another kind of restriction with hard work, determination, and the help of an unusual research team at Wright State University.

12

One Step at
a Time

When Nan Davis graduated from Wright State University in Dayton, Ohio, in 1982, the audience cheered as she took a few awkward steps to the stage. Nan had not walked since the night of her high school graduation in 1978 when a car accident left her legs paralyzed. The cheers were not for a miraculous recovery, but for Nan's courage and effort. Those tentative steps also represented years of patient, plodding research by an uncommonly dedicated team of scientists and engineers at Wright State's National Center for Rehabilitation Engineering (NCRE), who shared in that day's wild applause.

Wright State is named for Orville and Wilbur Wright, whose inventiveness and determination allowed people to fly. There's a satisfying logic in the fact that this center was created by Dr. Jerrold S. Petrofsky, a man as inventive and determined as the Wright brothers. During the fourteen years of work that led up to Nan

Davis's dramatic computerized walk, Dr. Petrofsky had made some discoveries about the use of electricity to stimulate the nerves that activate muscles.

Without thinking about it, we move because our muscles respond to electrochemical messages from nerve cells. It's a two-way system, with feedback to the brain to let us know what's happening. A burned finger hurts because the sensory message zips to the brain, which then stimulates the muscles to move the finger away from the heat, all faster than it takes to tell about it. If the connection is broken between nerves and muscles, it's like a cut phone line. The message can't get through and the muscles can't respond. When the spinal cord is damaged, the legs are paralyzed because the message can't get from the brain to the legs and back again.

There is no cure for paralysis caused by such broken connections.

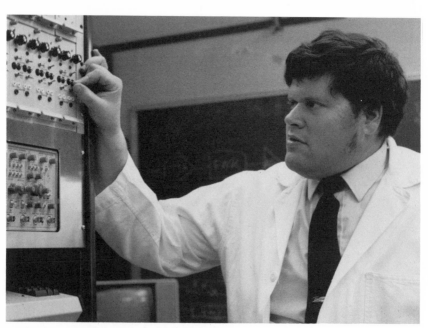

Jerrold S. Petrofsky, Ph.D., was executive director of the National Center for Rehabilitation Engineering when he developed a system of computer-assisted movement for paralyzed muscles. *(Wright State University, Dayton, Ohio)*

Millions of Americans are victims of paralysis from strokes, cerebral palsy, muscular dystrophy, spinal injuries, or any number of other neurological disorders. The National Spinal Cord Injury Foundation reports between ten and fifteen thousand spinal cord injuries annually resulting in paralysis, mostly from car accidents, with the majority of victims between the ages of eighteen and thirty. It's a conservative estimate because the statistics are taken from surveys only of paraplegics who are in hospitals or in some kind of rehabilitation program.

Along with the personal agony, there is an enormous financial burden. Being paralyzed costs a fortune. It is estimated that the initial hospitalization after a car accident costs more than $200,000, with an added $100,000 each year just to keep going. Over a lifetime it may cost two or three million dollars to care for a

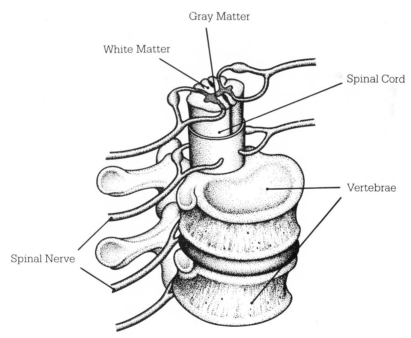

The spinal cord and connecting spinal nerves are protected by the vertebrae.

paraplegic, who frequently has a shortened life expectancy because he or she is easy prey to infections and diseases.

Dr. Ralph Stacy, a senior scientist on the Wright State staff, said, "Imagine being stuck in a wheelchair. You may feel fine. You still like the same foods, the same music, the same sports, the same friends. You haven't changed much, but you're stuck. You need help to go anywhere or do the most ordinary things. It doesn't take long before your unused muscles begin to deteriorate. Your bones break as easily as toothpicks because they lose calcium rapidly when they're not used. Knowing there is no cure, you'd be excited about a way to help yourself back to strength and self-sufficiency, which is what our research here is doing."

Dr. Petrofsky spent years watching, measuring, and testing cats to see precisely how their muscles worked. From all the data he collected, Dr. Petrofsky created computer programs that would do the "thinking" for muscles. At Wright State, he joined forces with Dr. Chandler Phillips and other scientists and technicians. When they were ready to try their electrical stimulation on people, they looked for volunteers. Unlike the very sick people who are the experimental patients for the artificial heart and various other transplants, the people Dr. Petrofsky wanted were young and relatively healthy, with enough upper body strength to take part in rigorous experiments.

Determined to walk again, Nan Davis met the requirements. As one of the first volunteers, Nan made spectacular news with her achievement because the story was so full of hope. The Wright State research group worried that the publicity also made it seem too dramatic and too easy and available to anyone. It is dramatic. It is not easy, and it is in the experimental stage, available only to a few.

The Wright State labs look as though a health club had moved into an electronics shop. They are packed with people and activity. A young man pedals an overgrown exercise bicycle they call "superbike." The only difference between it and an ordinary stationary bike is the seat arrangement, designed to hold a paraplegic or quadraplegic who has no control over his posture. Several wires glued to the rider's thighs lead to the computer, which substitutes for the brain in relaying signals to the nerves that stimulate the muscles. The rider's high sneakers, called "break away" shoes, are fastened to the pedals by Velcro pads so they can easily come off to prevent injury. The young man is not just strapped into a machine with the machine moving his legs. This is quite different from most physical therapy in which the legs or arms are moved passively. Because the electrical stimulation is telling the nerves to make the paralyzed muscles move, this young man is doing the work—and it is hard work as he pedals fifty revolutions per minute with varying loads on the flywheel.

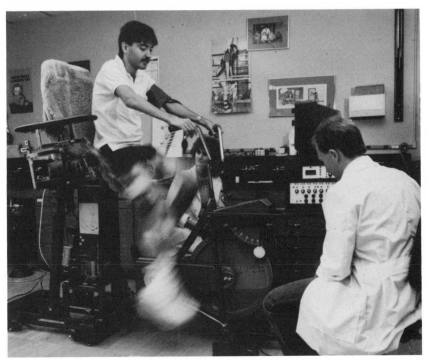

With the help of a programmed electrical stimulation–computerized feedback system, George Beyer, who is a paraplegic, pedals the exercise bike to strengthen his leg muscles. *(Wright State University, Dayton, Ohio)*

The important part of this computer-controlled system is its "closed loop," which means that information goes two ways. Sensors on the body tell the computer both the position and the movement of the muscle, and adjustments can be made to minimize muscle fatigue and stress on joints and bones.

On a body exerciser for the first time since he lost the use of his legs seven years ago, another young man begins his first session of active physical therapy. In spurts of one-thirtieth of a second, 125 milliamperes of electricity send signals to the nerves that control his leg muscles. His leg lifts. It's hooked to a cable with a two-pound weight pulling back. By the time he has finished four weeks in this series, he'll be pulling eighteen to twenty pounds, which will build both muscle size and strength. In time, with consistent workouts, it is possible that his thin, useless legs could look as they did before his accident, or maybe better.

A technician warns that there's always a temptation to try too much at first. Because the paraplegic or quadraplegic doesn't feel anything, he can't know if the weight is too much to bear. The technician must keep within prescribed limits as he monitors the amount of extension of the limb. The force could easily break the bones, and this young man wouldn't even know.

One of the major problems for people with paralysis is the unknown broken bone. Like astronauts in spaceflights who lose calcium at zero gravity, we earthbound people lose calcium unless there is constant vertical stress on our bones. One of the reasons older people are encouraged to keep walking and exercising is to avoid this loss of calcium common to those elderly who instead choose to retire to a rocking chair. A paraplegic can lose up to 75 percent of hard bone density simply because the bones aren't being used.

Another hidden danger for paraplegics and quadraplegics is overheating. With loss of motor and sensory nerves, all automatic functions, including sweat glands, are lost below the level of the injury. Body temperature can soar suddenly while working on the equipment without proper controls.

The combination of aerobic and isotonic exercise causes muscles to change length while moving a weight, just as they do in jogging or bicycling. It conditions the heart, improves muscular endurance, and strengthens the lungs. Many weight lifters are strong, but they have little endurance. Many long-distance runners have endurance but low strength. The goal of these paraplegics is endurance *and* strength. People who have been paralyzed for ten years or more have improved their muscular strength to near normal in a few months with these progressive resistance exercises. A wonderful and exhilarating side effect of the experiments has been the restored self-esteem of these wheelchair-bound volunteers.

Nan Davis started, as all the Wright State volunteers do, by lifting weights with her legs fifteen minutes a day, three days a week. She graduated to workouts on the bike, and then one day Dr. Petrofsky decided it was time for her to try to walk. Before her first attempt, long hours were spent programming into the computer the information necessary for each muscle movement and wiring the circuits that would relay the messages.

Trussed into a parachute harness that made her look like an awkward puppet suspended from a frame, Nan was hoisted to her feet. The harness, which offset some of Nan's weight, was a safety device used in that early system. She gripped the handrails, and the computer sent the first signals to her nerves. Her legs jerked forward, and everyone cheered. It was not only Nan's first step since her accident, but it was also the first step in a long series of refinements and adjustments that Petrofsky's team would make to improve the system.

The huge computer needed to trigger Nan's first steps has been reduced to a small, battery-powered pack worn at the waist. With the help of a team at NCRE, it is being further miniaturized, and specialists at Louisiana State University have made strong, indi-

Nan Davis, who is a paraplegic, stands under her own muscle power with the assistance of a computer at Wright State University's National Center for Rehabilitation Engineering in Dayton, Ohio. Since this photograph was taken in 1982, many changes have been made in the computer-assisted walking system. *(Wright State University, Dayton, Ohio)*

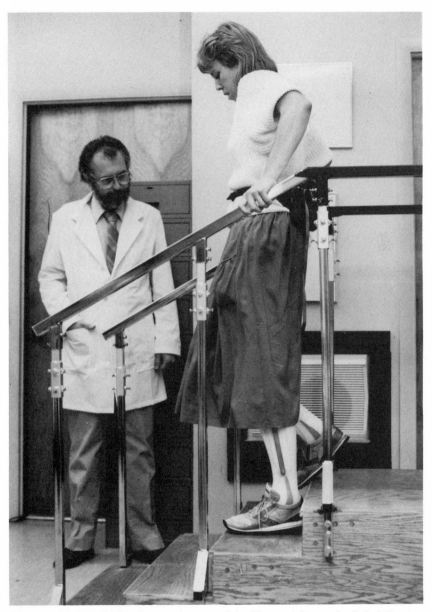

Chandler Phillips, M.D., deputy director of the National Center for Rehabilitation Engineering, watches Nan Davis demonstrate a newer computer-controlled walking system that permits her to use steps and ramps as well as walk backward or forward. *(Wright State University, Dayton, Ohio)*

vidually fitted braces that give the walker more stability while the muscles are stimulated to move the legs. The person can go forward or backward or turn around at the touch of a switch, but the braces are built so that if the electronics fail, the person can walk a short distance supported by the brace and canes or a walker. It's not unusual to see one of the paraplegic volunteers taking a computer-assisted walk across campus or shopping at a mall.

The new hybrid walking system, which includes the computer-controlled feedback developed at Wright State University and a lightweight brace made at Louisiana State University, allows paraplegics Gene Leber *(left)*, Nan Davis *(center)*, and Jennifer Smith *(right)* to get around the campus without wheelchairs. *(Wright State University, Dayton, Ohio)*

Even the wires are streamlined. Instead of waiting for the tedious gluing on of the surface electrodes, a person can pull on undergarments that Dr. Stacy said the volunteers call "hot pants," which have the electrodes built in at the proper places. The Petrofsky team uses surface electrodes, believing they work best, at least with the present technology. Other labs are working on implantable electrodes, but infection and other problems must still be overcome before they will be ready for widespread use.

Wright State's National Center for Rehabilitation Engineering has a variety of other projects, including bone-density studies, which have resulted in a device for "artificial walking." It is a vibration platform that mimics the impact on a bone of walking, with the intention of stimulating the bone in a paralyzed limb to deposit more calcium.

Another device being developed at the Wright State lab is a hand-control system that can help quadriplegics grip objects with their paralyzed hands. A tape recorder-sized control box mounted on the wheelchair connects by wires to electrodes in the sleeve of a shirt. Sensors are attached to the shoulder area, and these detect slight shoulder movements, which activate the electrical stimulation of the arm muscles and allow the person to close his hand more firmly as he picks up an object. Simple personal chores such as combing hair or holding a fork are major problems for a person with paralyzed arms. This hand-control system gives these people greater independence, and simple tasks once again become simple for them.

Some people are only partially paralyzed, with perhaps a weakened hand, arm, or leg. The Wright State group is developing a neural-boost system which will do just that—give a boost to the nerves by amplifying the electrical signals that the brain sends to the partially paralyzed limb.

"We get thousands of letters from paralyzed people looking for help. Unfortunately we can accept only a few," Dr. Stacy said,

The hand-control system developed at Wright State University to help quadraplegics grip objects more firmly is demonstrated by Susan Steele, who is a student and volunteer at the National Center for Rehabilitation Engineering. *(Wright State University, Dayton, Ohio)*

"and we're looking for people who have realistic expectations. We don't offer a cure. This is still an experimental program, and we have rigid criteria for our volunteers."

Some of the equipment, such as the whole body exerciser and the tricycle, is now used in hospitals, nursing homes, and rehabilitation centers, and will soon be available for home use, too. But the National Center for Rehabilitation Engineering states emphatically in its publications: "Functional electrical stimulation of muscle is not a cure. It is a method of rehabilitating people with paralysis to help improve their health, appearance, and psychological outlook and to return some mobility to their paralyzed muscles through external means. It is one answer that is not intended to replace the search for final cures, but is intended to work in concert with research to totally reverse paralysis. It offers a way to help paralyzed individuals rebuild their health and strength, so that when a cure is found, their bodies will be conditioned to withstand the rigors of regained motion."

Dr. Petrofsky is more direct. "Picture yourself as a twenty-year-old person who has just been told you will never walk again and the physical condition of your body will deteriorate with each passing day. Imagine the anger and loss you will feel. For such a person, the knowledge that a cure might be found someday is little consolation. What that person wants to know is what can scientific research do for me *today*? At NCRE we spend a great deal of time with people in wheelchairs. We recognize their sense of urgency, and we share it."

13

New Parts for
Old Brains

You can have electronic arms, artificial legs, a plastic heart, and transplanted lungs, liver, or kidneys. You don't need your own teeth or hair, and you can survive with a rebuilt skin. With all these new parts, you would still be you.

But who would you be with another brain in your skull?

Your brain is you. It is your mind that generates all your thoughts, emotions, senses, and responses. It's hard to imagine any situation in which a brain transplant ever would be considered, but what if it were possible to replace a specific part of the brain—a portion damaged by disease, for example?

We are born with about a hundred billion brain cells. Only ten billion of these are the neurons, the cells that send and receive the messages. Each neuron is made up of a petunia-shaped cell body with a long, drawn-out tail called an axon. Dendrites branch from the cell body like twigs on a tree. In spite of the enormous number of dendrites and axons, they never quite touch one another. The space between them is called the synaptic cleft, and that space is an important part of the message system. Billions of glial cells surround the neurons like glue. They supply nourishment and support but seem to have no part in the transmission of messages. All information in the brain is processed by electrical impulses and chemicals.

A pain, a sight, or a message from any of the body's organs is sent from the neuron's cell body and out along the axon. When it reaches the synaptic cleft at the end of the axon, it has to change vehicles. It's like driving across an island in a car and then getting into a boat to continue the trip across the river to land on the other side. In the case of the neuron, the message changes from the vehicle of the electrical impulse on the axon to the vehicle of a chemical for crossing the synaptic gap. This chemical messenger, called a neurotransmitter, "docks" at the next axon or dendrite by fitting into a space called a receptor site. It's a very specific, reserved space. Like one key for one lock, each neurotransmitter fits into one receptor site. The chemical vehicle changes back to an electrical impulse and continues on its way through an incredibly complex circuit. Only one kind of neurotransmitter is usually involved in the transmission of information within one of these circuits.

About eighty neurotransmitters have been discovered, although some scientists think there may be more than five hundred. Among the first found, and the ones we hear most about, are acetylcholine (ACH), serotonin (5-HT), norepinephrine (NE), and dopamine (DA).

Under normal conditions we lose perhaps 50,000 neurons a day, and more may be damaged through disease or stroke or head injuries or the use of alcohol and other drugs. These neurons are not replaced. Sometimes we can learn to develop new connections or pathways for interrupted messages, but we don't rebuild the old ones. A neurologist has described the brain's communication network as a long-distance phone line. You can make a direct call from New York to San Francisco. If that line is cut, your call can be rerouted through other cities. It might go through Chicago, Las Vegas, and several small towns in California before it gets to San Francisco. Your call will be completed, but it might not be as fast or as clear a connection. A patient recovering from brain injury may not be able to make that fast, clear, direct connection and will have to learn a new route. If speech has been hampered through stroke or carbon monoxide poisoning, for example, the patient may learn to talk again, but it may be slower, more deliberately thought out, and perhaps not as clear because of the rerouted connection. Unfortunately, there are times when no amount of relearning can alter the connections of damaged brain tissue.

For a long time, the brain was thought to operate as a whole, in which case it wouldn't do any good to repair a few cells here and there. Even after neurotransmitters were discovered, the brain was still thought of as a computerlike system that had to operate as a unit. Then researchers began to ask, if the loss of a few neurons could cause disorders, could the addition of a few neurons fix them? The answer was yes.

Unlike the body's other organs, which are protected by the immune system, the brain is "immunologically privileged." That means no antibodies rush to fight off the foreign invaders, or if they do, it's a delayed attack. That lack of "fight" has made it possible for a new patch of implanted cells to replace those destroyed by disease.

Like all good research scientists, Dr. Don Marshall Gash at the University of Rochester (New York), who is one of the pioneers of nerve cell transplantation, reviewed the early research before he began experiments in the late 1970s. He found that in 1903 Elizabeth Hopkins Dunn, a research assistant in a lab at the University of Chicago, had successfully transplanted neurons from ten-day-old rats into their littermates. Several of the grafts lasted sixty-six days. For some reason, Dr. Dunn waited ten years before she published her findings, and another thirteen years went by until the next significant studies on similar transplants appeared.

An experiment that Dr. Gash calls an example of a "premature and ill-founded human study" took place in 1942, when a surgical group in St. Louis grafted a section of spinal cord into a sixteen-year-old boy with a spinal cord injury. The transplanted piece had been removed from a body during autopsy two weeks earlier and stored in a solution of 70 percent ethanol. A three-inch section of the cadaver cord was "glued" into the gap between the cut ends of the patient's cord. About four months later the patient died. "No positive effects of the transplantation were reported," wrote Dr. Gash.

But several other experiments in the 1940s showed that it was possible to graft brain cells from one species to another. Guinea pigs with human brain-cell grafts were alive and well for more than two years when the experiments were ended. After that, however, brain research appeared to be "on hold" until the 1970s, when the whole concept of the nervous system seemed to undergo radical changes that caused renewed interest in the field.

For his first successful brain implant experiments, Dr. Gash used a mutant strain of rats born with defective neurons that caused them to have diabetes. Like humans who are diabetic, these rats could not maintain a normal balance of fluids. They were always thirsty and often drank their weight in water in a day. After implants of microscopic bits of healthy brain tissue from the embryos of rats without diabetes, the diabetic rats no longer had the symptoms. These implants worked so well that the research team was encouraged to try other repairs. This time their target was Parkinson's disease, a disorder that afflicts more than half a million people in the United States alone. It causes patients to lose control of muscles; their hands and limbs shake, and their walk slows to a shuffle. In advanced cases, patients have difficulty swallowing and speaking.

Parkinson's disease, first described by James Parkinson in 1817, is caused by a loss of neurons in a circuit that uses dopamine as a neurotransmitter. By replacing a patient's low supply of dopamine with a drug called L-dopa, it is possible to partially control the tremors. Unfortunately, L-dopa's effects gradually lose their punch. Larger doses are necessary, but an overdose can cause the patient to lose control, with extreme shaking of head and limbs.

Researchers thought that if some of the damaged dopamine-producing neurons could be replaced, the results might be as good or better than the drug's, and they were. Again, rats were the experimental models. By injecting the rats with a toxic substance that destroyed the brain's center of dopamine production, called the substantia nigra, it was possible to produce symptoms similar to Parkinson's disease. When implants of dopamine-producing neurons replaced the damaged brain cells, the rats began to walk normally again. As the implanted cells began to produce dopamine, the symptoms of Parkinson's disappeared. A key to the success of these grafts was the use of immature brain cells. Fetal and embryonic tissue works best and grows most successfully in an older host.

The next step was trying the same implants on primates, also using fetal tissue. But it didn't work very well. Out of dozens of implants, only one sprouted new nerve fibers. Even if fetal cell implants had worked, most researchers felt they couldn't have applied such implants to humans anyway. To use brain tissue from human fetuses would be ethically impossible.

When they looked for another source of dopamine-producing tissue, the researchers turned to the walnut-sized adrenal glands, which sit right on top of the kidneys. The small amount of dopamine made by the adrenals is used in the manufacture of the "fight or flight" hormones, adrenalin and noradrenalin. Bits of adrenal tissue taken from rats with symptoms of Parkinson's were implanted in the rats' brains. It worked, not as well as the fetal tissue, but with enough success to try the procedure in primates.

Now the problem was creating Parkinson's symptoms in the monkeys, and a terrible mistake in a "heroin kitchen" provided an answer. In 1982, drug addicts in San Francisco began showing up in emergency rooms unable to move. One patient could move only his eyes. While the physicians were doing everything they could to help the man, Dr. J. William Langston, a neurologist at Stanford University Medical School, noticed that the patient's symptoms were like those seen in extreme cases of Parkinson's. The paralyzed man was given an injection of L-dopa, and the result was dramatic. The patient got up and walked away. That drug addict, and many others, had taken an illegal "designer drug," probably from an underground chemist trying to make a synthetic heroin called MPPP. By using an apparently incorrect formula, he got a by-product called MPTP, which damages the substantia nigra, the area of the brain affected in Parkinson's. The FDA confiscated the dangerous drug, but when researchers worked with it further, they found that the drug could mimic the symptoms of Parkinson's disease in rats. As surely as if they had used a scalpel to cut out the dopamine-using circuit, the drug turned these rats into Parkinson's "patients." It also worked in monkeys.

The usual order of research progresses from perfecting a technique in rats, then moving up to larger mammals, to eventually trying the method on nonhuman primates before tests on humans. While American scientists were following this plan, a team at the Karolinska Institute in Sweden had jumped ahead in 1982 to graft adrenal cells into human brains.

Lacking a good primate model for Parkinson's, Dr. Lars Olson, a tissue specialist at Karolinska, along with neurosurgeons on the team, decided it would be unethical *not* to try these transplants on Parkinson's patients who were almost beyond hope of help in

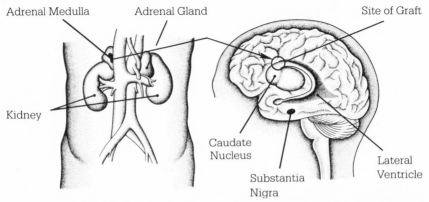

Adrenal Medulla   Adrenal Gland   Site of Graft

Kidney

Caudate
Nucleus
                                                     Lateral
                        Substantia   Ventricle
                        Nigra

The group of cells in the brain called the substantia nigra produces dopamine. Parkinson's disease occurs when these cells die. Grafts of dopamine-producing cells from the medulla, or core, of the adrenal glands into the brain's lateral ventricle can reverse the symptoms of Parkinson's.

any other way. They had three criteria: the patients had to be relatively young; they must have had no dementia so they could be fully informed about the experiment; and all usual therapy must have failed. By 1985, three men and one woman had received the grafts. (Most scientists prefer the terms "graft" or "implant" because brain transplant implies some kind of Frankenstein experiment and because they are dealing with a very small number of cells.) These grafts did not result in a miracle cure. None of the patients became suddenly healthy, but all of them improved dramatically, at least for a while. It's a start. Dr. Olson says that at least they know they are getting the right compounds to the right places, and the experiments have given an enormous boost to all brain-graft research.

The Swedish "guinea pigs" donated their own adrenal tissue, which not only eliminates any possibility of even a delayed rejection, but is also easily done. Taking a piece from one of the pair of adrenals is not dangerous because the other increases its hormone production to make up for it.

Dr. Don M. Gash found another source of neural transplant

material in cells cultured from a form of nerve cancer called a neuroblastoma, found mostly in young children. After the tumor is removed during surgery, the cells are treated to render them benign. Implanted in the brains of African green monkeys, the cells have survived for nine months without reverting to their cancerous condition.

One of the most totally destructive and terrifying diseases of the brain is Alzheimer's. It's been called the "disease of the century" and the "silent epidemic" because it strikes so many so unaware. It is diagnosed by the process of elimination, and there is no known cure. In 1906, the German neurologist Alois Alzheimer examined the brain of a fifty-one-year-old woman who had died after years of increasing loss of memory and control of her body, until she no longer could care for herself at all. He discovered in her brain clumps of twisted nerve-cell fibers that he called "neuro-fibrillary tangles." For years after this condition was identified as a specific disease, many people continued to call any kind of decreased brain function in old age simply senile dementia, or senility.

One of the important things that's come from research on Alzheimer's is the fact that senility is not a normal part of aging. It is true that the body slows down, hearing diminishes, eyes cloud from cataracts, bones lose calcium, and muscles may become weak as we grow older. And while it is also true that we can't replace the brain cells lost over the years, new research shows that the dendrites continue to grow. It's as though the more we learn and the more we use our brains, the richer and denser the connections get. Even though older people may experience some annoying loss of short-term memory, such as where they put the keys or whether they took their pills, they never really stop learning.

Further research found in the brains of Alzheimer's victims clumps of degenerated nerve endings called plaques along with the tangled fibers. The more plaques and tangles, the worse the disease. Diagnosis is difficult because the brain is redundant, which means that it "covers up" its own weakness as other parts of the brain take over the work of injured or worn-out cells. Until 80 percent of the brain is affected with these tangles and plaques, there may be no sign of the disease at all. Symptoms can take ten or fifteen years to appear, and when they do, it's too late to do anything about it.

In 1976, scientists at three labs in England came up with the same information; they found that Alzheimer's patients have a very low level of an enzyme responsible for making the neurotransmitter acetylcholine (ACH). Other neurotransmitters are involved, too, but the ACH seems to be the key. It is normally produced deep inside a small area of the brain called the nucleus basalis. Autopsies on the brains of Alzheimer's victims show a loss of neurons in this area.

One of the reasons it is so difficult to track Alzheimer's is the fact that the disease isn't localized in one part of the brain, as is Parkinson's. Nobody knows where or how it starts. Is it a slow virus that can lie dormant for years before causing symptoms? Is it genetic?

Early in 1987, researchers at the National Institute of Neurological and Communicative Disorders and Strokes found a gene responsible for the abnormal plaques and tangles that clog the brains of Alzheimer's victims. This gene contains the genetic information that triggers the production of a large protein that is modified into smaller proteins that form the disastrous tangles. It was found on chromosome 21, which is known to hold the genetic information linked to Down's syndrome. But the big question remains, do these plaques and tangles cause Alzheimer's, or are they the result of the disease?

At Albert Einstein College of Medicine in New York, researchers are looking for ways to replenish the brain's ACH and other neurotransmitters. At Dartmouth Medical School, a chemical called bethanechol chloride has been found that imitates the action of ACH, but it's difficult for a patient to get enough of the drug when it is given orally. So Dr. Robert E. Harbaugh and his team have devised a small pump that can be implanted under the skin of the abdomen. The pump feeds a slow, steady dose of bethanechol chloride into the brain through a tiny tube. So far, the patients on whom this technique has been tested have shown some improvement. But it's not a cure.

The hope is that a small brain tissue transplant could reverse Alzheimer's, or at least stop it from raging through the brain. The problems seem almost insurmountable because the disease invades so many parts of the brain and involves so many neurotransmitter systems. But Dr. Gash and his team in Rochester, the research group in Sweden, and others are working on it.

Every family in America will probably be affected by some neurological disorder at some time. According to the National Institutes of Health, there are up to sixteen million Americans who are deaf or hard of hearing. Ten million have impaired vision that cannot be corrected by glasses or contact lenses, and between two and four million people have epilepsy or are disabled by strokes. Millions more suffer from senile dementia, including Alzheimer's disease, and perhaps half a million have Parkinson's.

There are now at least nine model systems of different neurological deficiencies in rats that can be corrected by using neural implants. It won't be long before these are adapted for human use. Beyond that, researchers will find out someday how nerve cells grow and regenerate. They will learn how to reestablish broken connections, restore the circuitry, or create a bridge over damaged neurons. Dr. Carl Cotman, at the University of California, Irvine, found that the brain cells of Alzheimer's victims try to repair the connections destroyed by the disease. Undamaged nerve fibers sprout as though they are trying to seek out target neurons, and Cotman sees this optimistically as a sign of some kind of "battle plan" within the brain against its destruction. The search is on for the growth- and survival-enhancing chemicals, the ones that in some way send signals, as though they're saying, "I want dopamine-producing cells and no others."

No one knows if brain grafts will ever become routine procedure, but every year there are more intricately designed experiments, better equipment, and more answers. Supersmall submicron particles have been developed that will make it possible to probe and track a single neuron, which may make all that's been done so far seem primitive by comparison.

14

The Secret of
the Salamander

How bionic will we be? How will bodies be repaired in the twenty-first century? What is on the leading edge of medical research today?

The future belongs to the infinitesimal. At the National Research and Resource Facility for Submicron Structures at Cornell University in Ithaca, New York, engineers are thinking supersmall, so small that they've engraved the entire *Encyclopaedia Britannica* on a postage stamp. They are working with matter, one atom at a time, using measurements as small as one micron, which is one millionth of a meter, about one-sixtieth of the diameter of a human hair.

The submicron lab looks like a massive bomb shelter. Strangely enough, the equipment for supersmall materials is enormous. It must be mounted on thick concrete slabs because footsteps can have the impact of an H-bomb on submicron particles. Dust in the air is devastating. Compared to a submicron particle, a speck of dust is a mountain. Anyone entering the lab goes first through an air lock. When the door opens, the whole laboratory "exhales" its higher-than-outside air pressure to keep debris in the outside air from getting in. Visitors and employees stick their feet into a shoe-cleaning machine and pull on plastic boots, smocks, and bonnets.

The lab is a Class 1000 clean room, which means that every cubic foot of air contains fewer than 1,000 particles of dust one-half micron in diameter or larger. Air found in the average office is Class 300,000. Around some of the most sensitive equipment in the submicron lab, the air is filtered to a Class 10 status.

Working with submicron particles is basic research at a level where, according to one researcher, it's difficult to tell if it's chemistry or physics. The infinitesimal particles they are making have unparalleled speed and sensitivity. An electrical engineer at Cornell has made sensors so small that they can tap into individual cells. His work may produce a way to spy on nerve cells to detect the minute changes across cell membranes and find out precisely how they communicate; or to probe a single cancer cell to find out how it grows; or to analyze a muscle while it's twitching. It could lead to the creation of artificial bones, organs, and joints with precise monitors, and perhaps even artificial neurons to replace damaged nerves. Microscopic silicon chips packed with hundreds of thousands of instructions will make electronic eyes or bionic hands so sensitive they might respond to a user's thoughts just as normal eyes and hands do. Surgical tools might be made to zero in on a single gene.

At Los Alamos National Laboratory in New Mexico, the infamous birthplace of the atom bomb, scientists have assembled HUMTRN (pronounced HYOOM-tran), which will be the ultimate laboratory animal, the research rat of the future. They call it a "living" computer with a data bank that can be packed with ten million pieces of information on what happens when any chemical substance enters the body. HUMTRN, short for human transport, is programmed to react as though the body were eating, breathing, sleeping, perspiring, eliminating waste, working, aging, developing sexually, or dying. With it, impossible experiments become possible.

HUMTRN had its start when Dr. Anthony Gallegos was commissioned to determine how radioactivity would affect the human body in a theoretical accident at a nuclear arms assembly plant. It was an almost impossible job. A thousand factors could change. What if it rained that day or if the wind changed? What if all the workers were young men, or a combined work force of young women and middle-aged men? What organs in what age groups would be damaged? How could you assess the changes hour by hour or minute by minute? Dr. Gallegos says it was like a stupendous video game with any combination of factors possible. Done with conventional computer programs, the study could not have examined all the possibilities.

A team of thirty biologists and computer scientists worked on the program that will allow them to interpret thousands and thousands of pieces of data that would take years to accumulate and analyze in ordinary laboratory experiments. With this kind of computer, drugs, for example, could be tested without the use of a single laboratory animal. The Los Alamos lab has also built HUMTRN's software "siblings," including CLIMAP for predicting worldwide climate changes; PLTGRO, a plant duplicate; RMNANT, a ruminant or cattle duplicate; AQAT, a model for a deep-water, algae-producing lake; and several others.

Biomedical science has an arsenal of techniques we barely imagined twenty years ago. When they broke the genetic code and learned how to clone cells, biologists also discovered how to alter the code itself in the DNA that tells the genes what to do. Gene therapy is a way of correcting inborn errors of nature by changing the genetic information that causes such inherited diseases as cystic fibrosis, hemophilia, and sickle-cell anemia. Of the estimated 3,000 disorders caused by single-gene defects, more than 200 can be diagnosed. Researchers think there are between 50,000 and 100,000 individual genes that determine how we're built, and they've mapped about 800 of those. By the year 2000 they hope to have a complete map of genes that will lead to better genetic tests and treatments.

When the Italian anatomy professor Luigi Galvani discovered the electrical activity in the muscles of frogs in his laboratory back in 1771, it opened up a whole new science. In the next two hundred years we found out how electrochemical messages are sent from neuron to neuron. We found, in fact, that life could not exist at all without the constant flow of ions across the membranes of the cells.

Here and there throughout the history of medicine, the idea of a human electrical system has been hinted at but never proved. Even when it was found that bones knit better with electrical stimulation, no one really knew why. Bjorn Nordenstrom, a noted radiologist at the prestigious Karolinska Institute in Stockholm, Sweden, believes he has found the biological equivalent of a closed electrical circuit in the body. He thinks the ebb and flow within this biologically closed electric circuit is switched on by an injury or infection or tumor, or even by the normal activity of the body's organs. He believes it is the foundation of healing and the trigger that alerts our defense mechanisms. Many scientists have decided to wait for more proof before accepting Nordstrom's ideas, but most agree that it is a hypothesis that could change the way we patch and repair our bodies.

Patches and spare parts, whether in cars or people, are seldom as good as the original. The best solution would be finding ways to help the body repair itself. If only we knew the secret of the salamander! Orthopedic surgeon Dr. Robert O. Becker, author of *The Body Electric*, believes the body's own electricity may hold the answer.

Why is it that some animals with nervous systems simpler than ours can make their own replacement parts? How does the salamander grow a new leg? How does a lizard replace a tail lost in battle with a hawk? What organizes the regrowth? What is the control factor? How does the key clump of cells called the blastema know that it must make a foreleg instead of a hind leg? Dr. Becker says, "It's as if a pile of bricks were to spontaneously rearrange itself into a building, becoming not only the walls, but windows, light sockets, steel beams, and furniture in the process." And he marvels at the fact that the salamander never makes a mistake.

In the larval stage, a salamander can regenerate a leg in thirty to forty days. An adult salamander can also regrow a limb, but it takes longer and the leg is usually shorter than the original. In frogs, the amount of regeneration depends upon the animal's stage of development. The younger the frog, the more complete will be the regrowth. As amphibians and reptiles mature, they lose the ability to regrow limbs, although some regeneration can be induced with a graft of neural cells, which transmit the necessary information to control the regrowth. To a varying degree, all living things share the ability to regenerate lost parts.

Working at the Children's Hospital in Sheffield, England, in 1974, Dr. Cynthia M. Illingworth reported that children up to the age of eleven can regenerate "trapped" fingers. A trapped or guillotined finger is one that has been caught in a car door, for example, or in some way cut off at the tip. The usual treatment for such an injury involved surgery and a long, painful treatment period, until an oversight resulted in a new and startling method.

According to Dr. Illingworth, "One day, owing to a misunderstanding, a child with a guillotine amputation of a fingertip, whom the Senior House Officer had intended to refer to a plastic surgeon, had the finger covered with a simple dressing, and in error was not seen again for several days. The finger was healing beautifully and there was eventually complete regrowth of the tip. We now know that this happens in young children." Her report goes on to tell how complete this healing is with the "nonintervention technique." The length, contour, and function of the finger is completely restored. Even the fingernail and the whorls that make the fingerprints return to normal. Adults cannot regenerate fingertips as children do.

Dr. Anthony L. Mescher, a professor of anatomy at Indiana University School of Medicine, who has been studying regeneration in salamanders, says that several facts have been established. First, the limb must be injured. A withered or paralyzed limb lost from disuse does not regenerate. Second, the wound must close itself with an epithelium, which is the layer of cells programmed to grow outward. It must *not* be closed surgically. In his experiments, Dr. Mescher found that if the epithelium is prevented from forming across the amputation, the salamander cannot grow a new limb. That seems to be the case in the trapped fingers of children, too. And third, nerve cells must be present.

We're a long way from a time when we might regenerate our damaged organs or limbs. In the meantime, we must face the problems of both the ethics and expense of spare parts for people. Who will get help, and who will pay for it?

Is it more important to build dramatic equipment like the artificial heart that benefits only a few, or to spend research money on ways to prevent heart disease? Is it more important to spend money on lung cancer research or on ways to keep people from smoking? Most experts agree that we should be spending at least as much on research to prevent disease as on making experimental life-prolonging equipment.

Children growing up in the 1930s and 40s were terrified by a disease known as infantile paralysis or poliomyelitis. Frightened parents kept children away from crowded public swimming pools and parks. Movie theaters and schools closed in cities where polio epidemics raged. Even the most isolated families knew someone who had been crippled by the dreaded disease. No one knew how it spread, and there was no cure. Hospital wards were lined with huge metal cylinders called "iron lungs" that kept paralyzed victims alive by forcing air in and out of their lungs. Then the polio virus was isolated, and Jonas Salk made the vaccine that now prevents it.

Like great metal dinosaurs, iron lungs became displays in medical museums, merely interesting antiques since polio was virtually wiped out. Perhaps the artificial heart will become an obsolete

In the 1940s, before the discovery of a vaccine to prevent poliomyelitis, an iron lung "breathed" for paralyzed victims of the disease. It was a useful spare part no longer necessary when research found a better way of controlling the disease. *(National Library of Medicine)*

museum piece, too, having served its purpose until better methods of heart repair are found. In the next twenty years, many lines of research that seem now to lead to solutions may be abandoned as others are picked up. Disease has had an enormous head start. It's been around for millions of years, while science has been searching for answers for only a tiny fraction of that time.

It is said that medical knowledge doubles every five years. Almost every day dramatic new developments are reported. A textbook published in 1980 would have no mention of the artificial heart, monoclonal antibodies, or the first successful heart-lung transplant. Five years in the future, we'll be reading about breakthroughs we cannot imagine now.

A scientist was once defined as a person with unconcealed curiosity, someone who asks, "Why?" An engineer asks, "How?" The "how" and the "why" researchers have combined forces. Bioengineers working with physicists, chemists, biologists, physicians, and surgeons are moving us into a medical revolution bound to change the way we live.

Glossary

ALLOGRAFT. Transplanted tissue that has been obtained from a human cadaver.

ANTIBODY. A protein produced by the lymphocytes that recognizes and destroys or inactivates a specific antigen.

ANTIGEN. A substance foreign to the body that stimulates the immune system to produce antibodies against it.

AORTA. The largest artery in the body. It carries oxygenated blood from the left ventricle of the heart to all parts of the body.

AORTIC VALVE. A one-way valve between the aorta and the left ventricle of the heart.

AUTOGRAFT. Tissue, such as skin, taken from a patient's own body.

AUTONOMIC NERVOUS SYSTEM. That part of the brain (medulla) and nerves that regulates life activities such as breathing and heartbeat.

AXON. The long fiber from a nerve cell that carries impulses away from the cell body. At its end are synaptic knobs that produce the neurotransmitters.

BIOCOMPATIBLE. Any material that can be placed in living tissue without causing an immune response or damage to surrounding tissue.

BIOPSY. The removal of a piece of living tissue for laboratory analysis.

BRAIN DEAD.   No activity in the cerebrum of the brain; determined by a flat brain wave on an electroencephalogram.

COLLAGEN.   A tough, elastic fibrous protein found in bones, skin, cartilage, tendons, and other connective tissue. Collagen comprises one-third of the body's protein.

DENDRITES.   The short branches of a nerve cell specialized to receive impulses and send them to the cell body.

DNA.   Deoxyribonucleic acid; the molecule in cells that contains genetic information in the form of a code.

EEG.   Electroencephalogram. A chart that shows the electrical changes in the brain, obtained through electrodes attached to the scalp.

ENZYME.   A protein that acts as a catalyst by increasing the rate of a chemical reaction.

EPITHELIAL TISSUE.   Tissue with closely packed cells covering the surfaces of the body and individual organs and lining all cavities of the body.

GENE.   A portion of a DNA molecule that contains the code to produce a specific effect in a cell.

GLYCOGEN.   A complex carbohydrate that is one of the major stored food substances in animals. It can be converted to glucose.

HETEROGRAFT.   Tissue taken from one species and transplanted to another.

IMPLANT.   Placement of an artificial material in a living organism.

LYMPH.   A colorless fluid carried by lymph vessels; made by blood plasma.

LYMPH NODES.   Structures located along major lymph vessels that filter impurities such as bacteria from the lymph and destroy them with phagocytes.

LYMPHOCYTE.   A white blood cell that produces antibodies and can recognize and destroy antigens.

MEMORY CELL.   A cell produced by the lymphocytes that remains in the system to provide long-term immunity against an antigen.

MYOELECTRIC.   Referring to the tiny electrical current or potential current produced when a muscle contracts.

NEURON.   A nerve cell; the only kind of cell that can carry an impulse.

NEUROTRANSMITTER.   A substance released from the ends of axons of a neuron that stimulates or inhibits impulses in adjoining neurons.

PACEMAKER.   A mechanism that controls and regulates the rate of the heartbeat.

PERIOSTEUM.   A fibrous sheath of connective tissue surrounding the bone. It carries blood vessels to nourish bone cells.

PHAGOCYTE.   A kind of white cell that destroys foreign material such as bacteria by engulfing it.

PLASMA.   The liquid portion of the blood, consisting mainly of water and dissolved substances; blood minus the blood cells.

PLASMA CELL.   One type of cell produced by B-lymphocytes. It produces antibodies.

PLATELET. A blood cell fragment that initiates the clotting of blood.

PULMONARY ARTERIES. The arteries that carry blood from the right ventricle of the heart to the lungs to be oxygenated.

PULMONARY VALVE. A one-way valve between the pulmonary artery and the right ventricle of the heart.

REGENERATION. The regrowth of a lost body part.

REJECTION. When the immune system, primarily the T-lymphocytes, destroys the transplanted tissue and its blood supply.

SQUAMOUS CELLS. A type of epithelial cell that is thin and flat and fits tightly to others, forming the outer layer of skin.

STROKE. Damage to the brain from a decreased blood supply; caused by blood clots, hemorrhage, or accumulation of deposits in the blood vessels.

SYNOVIAL FLUID. A lubricating fluid that lines the inner surfaces of joints.

T-CELL. A type of lymphocyte that is produced in the bone marrow but that matures in the thymus gland. It makes antibodies that remain on the surface of a cell. It is the main part of the immune system, responsible for the rejection of tissue transplants.

THYMUS GLAND. A gland in the chest beneath the breastbone that is an active part of the immune system.

THYROID GLAND. The endocrine gland in the neck; produces a hormone that regulates the body's metabolism.

TRANSPLANT. The placement of living material into an organism, either from a different area of that same organism or from another organism.

UMBILICAL CORD. The cord that supplies oxygen and nourishment from the mother to the unborn baby. It contains two arteries and one vein.

Bibliography

Asimov, Isaac. *Biographical Encyclopedia of Science and Technology*. New York: Avon Books, 1976.

Becker, Robert O., M.D., and Gary Selden. *The Body Electric*. New York: William Morrow and Company, 1985.

Borgens, Richard B. "Mice Regrow the Tips of Their Foretoes." *Science*, Vol. 217, No. 456 (August 1982), pp. 747–750.

DeVries, William C., M.D., and Lyle D. Joyce, M.D., Ph.D. "The Artificial Heart." *Clinical Symposia*, Vol. 35, No. 6, 1983.

Donahue transcript #03065. Multimedia Entertainment, Inc., Cincinnati, Ohio, 1984.

Dossick, Philip. *Transplant, A Family Chronicle*. New York: The Viking Press, 1978.

Duerlinger, Jean. "Computerized Human Body Advances Ecology Research." *New York Times*, November 12, 1985.

Freese, Arthur S., M.D. *The Bionic People Are Here*. New York: McGraw-Hill Book Company, 1979.

Gash, Don Marshall. *Neural Transplants in Mammals, A Historical Overview*. Rochester, N.Y.: Department of Anatomy, University of Rochester School of Medicine and Dentistry, 1984.

Gohlke, Mary, with Max Jennings. *I'll Take Tomorrow*. New York: M. Evans and Company, 1985.

Greatbatch, Wilson. *Implantable Active Devices*. Clarence, N.Y.: Greatbatch Enterprises, 1983.

Halacy, D. S., Jr. *Cyborg: Evolution of the Superman*. New York: Harper & Row Publishers, 1965.

Hellerstein, David. "The Promise of Artificial Skin." *Science Digest,* Vol. 39, No. 9 (September 1985), pp. 62–79.

Illingworth, Cynthia M., M.D. "Trapped Fingers and Amputated Finger Tips in Children." *Journal of Pediatric Surgery,* Vol. 9, No. 6 (December 1974), pp. 853–857.

Jacobsen, Stephen C., David F. Knutti, Richard T. Johnson, and Harold H. Sears. "Development of the Utah Artificial Arm." *IEEE Transactions on Biomedical Engineering,* Vol. BME-29, No. 4 (April 1982), pp. 249–269.

Jarvik, Robert K. "The Total Artificial Heart." *Scientific American,* Vol. 244, No. 1 (January 1981), pp. 74–80.

Johnson, Stephen L. *The History of Cardiac Surgery*. Baltimore: The Johns Hopkins Press, 1970.

Knapp, Barbara, R.N., and William R. Panje, M.D. "A Voice Button for Laryngectomies." *Association of Operating Room Nurses,* Vol. 36, No. 2 (August 1982), pp. 183–193.

Langone, John. "Monoclonals: The Super Antibodies." *Discover,* Vol. 4, No. 6 (June 1983), pp. 68–72.

Leinwald, Gerald. *Transplants, Today's Medical Miracles*. New York: Franklin Watts, 1985.

Loeb, Gerald. "The Functional Replacement of the Ear." *Scientific American,* Vol. 254, No. 2 (February 1985), pp. 104–111.

Lynch, Wilfred. *Implants: Reconstructing the Human Body*. New York: Van Nostrand Reinhold Company, 1982.

Madison, Arnold. *Transplanted and Artificial Body Organs*. New York: Beaufort Books, 1981.

Malecki, Mindy S. "A Personal Perspective: Working With Families Who Donate Organs and Tissues." A news release from Rush–Presbyterian–St. Luke's Medical Center, Chicago, Illinois.

Maugh, Thomas H., II. "The Healing Touch of Artificial Skin." *Technology Review,* Vol. 88, No. 1 (January 1985), pp. 48–56.

Mescher, Anthony L. "Neurotrophic control of events in injured forelimbs of larval urodeles." *Journal of Embryology and Experimental Morphology,* Vol. 69 (1982), pp. 183–192.

Mowbray, A. Q. *The Transplant*. New York: David McKay Company, 1974.

Nassif, Janet Zhum. *Medicine's New Technology*. New York: Arco Publishing, 1980.

Paget, Stephen. *The Surgery of the Heart.* London: John Wright, 1896.

Porzio, Ralph. *The Transplant Age.* New York: Vantage Press, 1969.

Salomon, Michel. *Future Life.* New York: Macmillan Publishing Company, 1983.

Schnitman, Paul A., and Leonard B. Shulman, editors. *Dental Implants: Benefit and Risk.* Bethesda: U.S. Department of Health and Human Services, 1980.

Shaw, Margery W., editor. *After Barney Clark: Reflections on the Utah Artificial Heart Program.* Austin: University of Texas Press, 1984.

Siyahi, Carol, editor. "Newsletter." National Center for Rehabilitation Engineering, Wright State University, Dayton, Ohio, Vol. 1, Nos. 1 and 2.

Sonstegard, David A., Larry S. Matthews, and Herbert Kaufer. "The Surgical Replacement of the Human Knee Joint." *Scientific American,* Vol. 238, No.1 (January 1978), pp. 44–51.

Taubes, Gary. "An Electrifying Possibility." *Discover,* Vol. 7, No. 4 (April 1986), pp. 22–37.

Walker, Peter S. "Joints to Spare." *Science 85,* Vol. 6, No. 11 (November 1985), pp. 56–57.

Warshofsky, Fred. *The Rebuilt Man, The Story of Spare-Parts Surgery.* New York: Thomas Y. Crowell Company, 1960.

Wertenbaker, Lael. *To Mend the Heart, The Dramatic Story of Cardiac Surgery and Its Pioneers.* New York: Viking Press, 1980.

Wolf, Edward D. "Advanced Submicron Research and Technology Development at the National Submicron Facility." *Proceedings of the IEEE,* Vol. 71, No. 5 (May 1983), pp. 589–600.

Index